Nick Swinmurn, Tony Hsieh, and Zappos

INTERNET BIOGRAPHIES™

Nick Swinmurn, Tony Hsieh, and Zappos

ERIN STALEY

ROSEN PUBLISHING
New York

Published in 2014 by The Rosen Publishing Group, Inc.
29 East 21st Street, New York, NY 10010

First Edition

Library of Congress Cataloging-in-Publication Data

Staley, Erin.
Nick Swinmurn, Tony Hsieh, and Zappos/Erin Staley.—
First Edition.
pages cm.—(Internet biographies)
Includes bibliographical references and index.
ISBN 978-1-4488-9529-8 (library binding)
1. Zappos.com (Firm)-History. 2. Electronic commerce—United States—History. 3. Entrepreneurship—Moral and ethical aspects. 4. Businesspeople—United States—Biography. 5. Swinmurn, Tony, 1973- 6. Hsieh, Tony. I. Title.
HF5548.325.U6S73 2013
381'.456870922—dc23
[B]

2012040916

Manufactured in the United States of America

CPSIA Compliance Information: Batch #S13YA: For further information, contact Rosen Publishing, New York, New York, at 1-800-237-9932.

Contents

INTRODUCTION

If you've ever shopped online for the perfect pair of basketball sneakers, the cutest couture heels, or the latest in eco-friendly sandals, you've probably run across Zappos. It's the billion dollar dot-com business that was started when Nick Swinmurn couldn't find a particular pair of shoes at a local mall in 1998. With the help of Tony Hsieh, an entrepreneur, investor, and eventually Zappos's chief executive officer (CEO), the two men built the world's largest shoe store, both on and off of the Internet.

As adolescents, Nick and Tony each had an entrepreneurial spirit. They wanted to create successful businesses. Through trial and error, and with the help of many along the way, Nick and Tony came together to build a legendary shoe company. Neither was crazy about shoes; however, they were crazy about customer service. The men designed Zappos to give customers what they wanted in a friendly and timely manner. How did Nick and Tony keep thousands of customers returning to Zappos? They wowed them by providing the best selection, unparalleled customer service, free shipping, a no-fuss money-back guarantee, and easy access to Zappos team members. Nick and Tony made sure the customers were wowed by "delivering happiness" to doorsteps across the United States.

Zappos, known for its unconventional company culture, is one of the leading e-tailers in the world. Founded in 1999, this Nevada-based company ships thousands of items each day.

As Zappos evolved, so did its priorities. Today, its number one branding focus is not selection, customer service, or even wowing the customer. It's about company culture. Nick and Tony believe that if the company culture is intact, then Zappos team members will be happy. Happy team members make for happy Zappos customers. How do Nick and Tony keep their company happy? They shower them with endless employee benefits and opportunities to give back to the community. They also live by the "work hard, play hard" philosophy. Zappos encourages its team members to be "a little weird" and participate in all sorts of company activities including tug-of-war, dance nights, costume parades, cookie decorating, and even Pie Your Boss Day. It's no wonder Zappos has been one of *Fortune* magazine's "Best Companies to Work For" since 2009.

While Nick Swinmurn and Tony Hsieh are at the height of their professional careers today, they had to overcome many struggles along the way. We'll take a look at the events that led to the success of Zappos and the lessons Nick and Tony learned in making Zappos the go-to company for online shopping. Finally, we'll look at how a commitment to company culture can turn an idea into a billion dollar company in less than ten years.

Chapter 1

Early Life, Education, and Entrepreneurial Adventures

Nicholas Swinmurn, who would someday became the founder of a leading dot-com business, was born in England in 1973. When he was seven years old, his family moved to the San Francisco Bay area in California. As Nick entered his teenage years, he developed an interest in owning his own business. He dreamed of being an entrepreneur and started a bicycle club and tennis club in his hometown. At the same time, he tried to convince his parents to open a surf shop. In the early 1990's, Nick graduated from high school and entered the University of California, Santa Barbara, to study film. It was here that he was introduced to the Internet and registered for an "ucsb .edu" e-mail address. Although the Internet was a popular tool for instant communication, Nick couldn't figure out how to use his new address and gave up.

San Francisco, where Nick Swinmurn grew up, is known for the Golden Gate Bridge, Alcatraz, and Chinatown. Its eclectic culture, cable cars, steep hills, and funky architecture make it one of the world's most popular destinations.

As a young man, Nick became a student of customer service. He learned how to take care of customers and figured out what worked and what didn't. For instance, Nick traveled with his boss selling vacuums door-to-door. If the customer did not buy a vacuum, his boss would leave the pile of dirt from the sales demonstration on the customer's floor. Nick quickly realized that it wasn't a good display of customer service. He drew upon this example as one of the lessons that became the foundation of Zappos.

Upon graduation in 1996, Nick spent a season selling group tickets for the San Diego Padres, a professional baseball team in California. He wanted to build his career but realized that getting promoted would take a long time. He decided to quit and move back to the Bay Area in pursuit of a better position. In 1997, Nick was reintroduced to the Internet as the sales marketing manager for Autoweb .com, a leading automotive online e-commerce site. Nick was excited to be working in a thriving industry, and he had the potential to be promoted quickly. However, his entrepreneurial interests peaked once more. If Autoweb could design an e-commerce business, so could he. It was about this time that Nick went shopping at a local mall. Within twenty-four hours, he had an idea that would eventually change the way people shop for shoes. With only nine months at Autoweb, Nick quit and founded the dot-com business we now know as Zappos.

On December 12, 1973, Tony Hsieh (pronounced "Shay") was born to immigrant parents from Taiwan. His parents had met at the University of Illinois as graduate students and were married. Soon after, they started a family. When Tony was five years old, his father, Richard Hsieh, accepted a position as a chemical engineer for Chevron in California. The Hsieh family moved to Lucas Valley, California, which is north of San Francisco.

Tony's parents had set high academic standards for Tony and his two younger brothers. His mother, Judy Hsieh, was a social worker. She had hoped Tony would one day attend the prestigious Harvard University and

From earthworms to shoes, Tony Hsieh has built a career on his entrepreneurial spirit. His desire to continue learning and evolving has brought him success, both personally and professionally.

become a doctor of medicine or academics. Tony's parents expected him to get straight A's and excel on the SAT college entrance exam. The SAT exam is usually taken when one is in high school, but Tony began taking the test as a middle schooler. When he wasn't doing homework or watching the hour a week of television his parents allowed, Tony was rehearsing one of his four musical instruments. He played the French horn, piano, violin, and trumpet. For each instrument, he rehearsed thirty minutes per weekday. In the summer and on weekends, he practiced for one hour per day per instrument. Tony found this rigid schedule to be boring, so he devised a plan. At 6:00 AM, he would wake up and head downstairs to the piano. He played a session he had previously recorded using his tape recorder. An hour later, Tony would return to his bedroom and play back a violin recording. What did he do during this free time? He had his nose in a book or was reading a *Boys' Life* magazine.

Music was not Tony's passion. He wanted to make money because he believed it would allow him to live life as he desired. On his ninth birthday, Tony became an entrepreneur. His first business was the world's largest

Earthworms, Tony Hsieh's first business venture, were once thought to be sacred creatures by ancient Egypt's Cleopatra. Their knack for plowing the earth has been known for centuries.

earthworm distribution company. At his request, Tony's parents bought him a box of mud, guaranteed to have at least a hundred worms. Tony had learned that a worm cut in half would regenerate itself, producing two worms. He counted on this fact to grow his business. Tony built a box in his backyard complete with chicken wire and mud. He fed raw eggs to his worms every day. After one month, Tony sifted through the soil only to discover there were no baby worms. In fact, there were no worms at all. He quickly discovered that the worms had either escaped or been eaten. Disappointed, Tony realized his business had gone bust.

Tony didn't let this failure stop him from his goal. He attempted garage sales with lemonade stands, newspaper routes, newsletters, greeting cards, and eventually, a button-making mail-order business. Tony made buttons for people all over the country and earned a profit of $200 a month. But over time, Tony grew bored. His business was taking too much of his free time, especially on weekends. He passed the button business on to his younger brother. Despite the routine, Tony was convinced that a mail-order business could be extremely profitable. This belief eventually led to his extraordinary success with Zappos.

As a high school student, Tony was invited by a teacher to take her computer science class. He had dabbled in computer programming in middle school and thought the course would look good on his college applications.

Soon, he was spending his lunch break and after-school hours in the computer lab. It didn't take long for Tony and his fellow computer programmers to figure out that the lab's modem line could call long-distance phone numbers. Although the teacher had received the phone bill, she assumed the approximate three hundred phone calls were a mistake. Tony and his friends were never caught, but the phone calls stopped immediately.

It was during this time that Tony figured out a way to design his class schedule around two things: what was needed for college applications and what would give him the lightest homework load. He wanted to maximize his free time, allowing for money-making possibilities. He worked as a video-game tester and then as a computer programmer. However, he missed having his own business. Tony attempted his second mail-order product—magic tricks. Only this time, his new company didn't have the same kind of success as the button-making business.

Although he had applied to eight universities, Tony fulfilled his parents' wish and attended Harvard University. Once again, he crafted his class schedule to maximize his free time. He watched endless hours of television and spent time with a close-knit group of friends who lived in his dormitory. Even though he rarely made it to classes, Tony kept his grades up by borrowing lecture notes for homework and exams. One particular Bible class appealed to Tony because the professor didn't give homework.

Founded in 1636, Harvard University, which Tony Hsieh attended, was named after its first benefactor, the minister John Harvard of Charlestown. It's considered one of the country's top schools.

However, the semester grade was based on the final exam. Out of a hundred possible topics, the professor warned his class he would randomly select five topics from the list on exam day. Each student would have to write five essays, one for each topic. The problem was that Tony hadn't done any of the reading. With only two weeks until the exam, Tony sent an online message to all of the enrolled students. He invited them to contribute three well-developed essays based on the topics from the list of a hundred. Once he had collected them all, Tony bound all of the essays into a study guide and sold copies to the participants. Each guide was $20. He learned that study groups and crowdsourcing were powerful and profitable business tools.

While Tony enjoyed college life, he still missed having his own business. In 1994, he decided to run the Quincy House Grille, a dormitory eating area on the Harvard University campus. Sanjay Madan, one of Tony's roommates, joined him. A city ordinance prevented fast-food chains from opening up close to campus, so Tony headed for the nearest McDonald's. He bought dozens of frozen hamburger patties and buns. He cooked them up at the Quincy House Grille and sold them for $3 each. It wasn't long before Tony grew tired of the hamburger pick-ups day after day. So, he tried a different approach—pizza. He had learned that pizzas were inexpensive to make, and he invested in pizza ovens. Tony's efforts were a hit and tripled the Grille's sales of the previous year.

One of his best customers was Alfred Lin. Alfred would buy two large pizzas at night. Tony and Sanjay thought he must be a very hungry Harvard student until they discovered, several years later, that Alfred was selling the slices to students in his dormitory.

During their days at Harvard, Sanjay introduced Tony to the World Wide Web. Tony found it to be an interesting concept, but he was a college senior and needed to focus on finding a well-paying job after graduation. In 1995, Tony graduated with a degree in computer science and was hired as a software engineer at Oracle Corporation in California. Sanjay was also recruited by Oracle, and together, they moved and found an apartment close to work. It didn't take long for Tony and Sanjay to grow weary of their monotonous nine-to-five jobs. The World Wide Web was becoming increasingly popular, and the business possibilities were endless. The idea of starting their own e-commerce business excited Tony and Sanjay. They put their talents together and planned a Web site business. Both men quit their Oracle jobs to start their business, but within one week, they realized they no longer wanted to make sales calls or design Web sites. It was time to look for something else.

LINKEXCHANGE

On a whim in 1996, Tony and Sanjay came up with the idea of cooperative advertising. They wanted to offer traffic-generating services to small Web sites. Owners would sign up for the free service and enter a special code into their Web page. Banner ads would automatically appear on their site. Every time someone visited the site, the owner would get credit. Over time, the credits added up, and LinkExchange would have enough advertisements to sell to larger corporations. Over a March weekend, Tony and Sanjay finished the computer programming for their new project. They contacted fifty Web sites. Over half were interested in the service. Within one week, they knew they were onto something big. More sites signed up over the course of five months. Both men knew LinkExchange was on the right track when they received an offer in August to sell the company for $1 million. After much consideration, Tony and Sanjay believed they would be in a position of strength if they could walk away from the deal. They counter-offered for $2 million dollars. It was declined, but they were more motivated than ever to make LinkExchange a success.

Between computer programming and responding to customer e-mails, Tony and Sanjay worked around the clock in their apartment-turned-headquarters. More business meant more help was needed. Visiting friends were put to work helping customers while Tony and Sanjay looked for other computer programmers. They added programmer Ali Partovi as a third partner. By December, LinkExchange received another offer to sell. This time it was from Yahoo for $20 million. Even though it was more money than they could've dreamed of, Tony, Sanjay, and Ali realized they were just starting their professional lives. They could afford to be risky and turn down the offer. Tony could already buy the things he wanted, but with LinkExchange, he was a part of something bigger than himself. Together, the three partners rejected the offer. They were sure LinkExchange had joined the big names in Internet start-up companies. They weren't the only ones to believe this. In May 1997, Sequoia Capital invested $3 million dollars in their company.

With more and more Web sites signing up for the LinkExchange service, the work environment became fast-paced. Growth was inevitable, and they needed more employees. Tony, Sanjay, and Ali added Alfred Lin, Tony's pizza customer, as the vice president of finance. In addition, LinkExchange needed more office space. They expanded throughout their office building and opened offices in Chicago and New York. By 1998, LinkExchange had over a hundred employees. Many of them were highly skilled but were not excited about growing the business. This was disheartening to Tony, and he, too, began to lose enthusiasm for the company he had cofounded. Later, this lesson would inspire him to create a work environment where employees were motivated by passion, not by a paycheck.

Dot-Com Businesses in the 1990s

The concept of sharing computer information began in the early 1960s, and by 1995, ambitious entrepreneurs could see a whole new world of opportunity online. They worked day and night creating and building dot-com businesses, many of which were located in Silicon Valley, California. Dot-coms offered everything from clothing to pet supplies. But these start-ups needed investment money to keep growing. Inspired by the overnight success of Amazon, eBay, Google, and Yahoo!, venture capitalists invested millions of dollars in dot-coms.

Many investors believed that if a business had a dot-com after its name, then it would be an instant money-maker. It was the age of the dot-com bubble (1995–2000). The NASDAQ stock market agreed and set a high price on dot-com shares. It appeared that Internet start-up businesses were headed for financial stardom. However, in the spring of 2000, the NASDAQ crashed, and the dot-com bubble burst. The stock value dropped dramatically. Investors lost millions of dollars. Over the course of two years, countless dot-com companies went out of business.

How did this happen? Dot-com businesses had been given too much money too fast. Their business plans couldn't keep up with the growth. Many

(continued on next page)

(continued from previous page)
could not develop products quickly enough or deliver good customer service. Their plans lacked the tried-and-true principles of successful businesses: know your business, understand your market, develop a solid product, create customer loyalty, and prepare a strategy for long-term profits. Only a handful of dot-coms adapted and survived.

Timing was on Tony's side. Microsoft offered to buy LinkExchange for $265 million. Ali, Sanjay, and Tony approved the sale, and the acquisition was official on November 6, 1998. Microsoft wanted all three men to stay on for at least a year. If Tony stayed, he would get $40 million. If he left before the year was up, he would receive only $32 million. In a moment of reflection, Tony listed the things that made him happy: creating, building, and growing. None of these things involved money or material goods. He was restless at LinkExchange, so he quit in order to pursue other happy ventures.

VENTURE FROGS

In August 1999, Tony stumbled upon the Marquee Historical Building in San Francisco. It was adding fourteen movie theaters, a gym, restaurant, and fifty-three residential lofts. With a Taco Bell down the street, Tony

Once a devoted Quincy House Grille customer, Alfred Lin became LinkExchange's vice president of finance. After the business was sold to Microsoft, Alfred and Tony Hsieh went on to create Venture Frogs.

knew it was his future home. He convinced many of his LinkExchange friends to become neighbors, including Alfred Lin. Together, this group of friends recreated a university dormitory setting, complete with entertainment and fast food.

It didn't take long for Tony and Alfred to get the itch to start a business. They decided to open a venture capital firm. On a dare, they named the investment firm Venture Frogs and collected $27 million from LinkExchange friends who wanted to invest. Although they were a small fund, Venture Frogs had ambitious plans. They purchased the restaurant in the Marquee Building, and it became the Venture Frogs Restaurant. Tony's parents, Richard and Judy Hsieh, managed the restaurant with its menu of specialty dishes named after dot-com businesses. Tony and Alfred also wanted to invest in twenty-seven Internet start-up companies. They even leased 15,000 square feet (1,394 square meters) of office space in the building for a Venture Frogs incubator. It would provide office space for their start-ups. Little did Tony and Alfred know that at the time, they were building a home for one of the most exciting start-up companies in the dot-com industry.

Chapter 2

An Idea to Run With

In 1998, Nick Swinmurn had been looking for Airwalk desert chukka boots at a local San Francisco Bay mall. If one store had the right size, it was the wrong color. If another store had the right color, it was the wrong style. Nick left empty-handed and went home to see if he could find what he wanted online. There were a number of dot-com shoe

Zappos added a new twist to the traditional methods of buying shoes in a store. With Nick's creativity and Tony's know-how, the two revolutionized shoe shopping with online convenience.

businesses, but they were extensions of brick-and-mortar stores. Their Web site inventory was limited to the size of their store's storage area. The brick-and-mortar stores could stock only a certain number of brands, colors, sizes, and styles. With some research, Nick discovered that one in three shoe sales were lost because of limited stock. If Nick couldn't find what he was looking for, then how would anyone else? And who wouldn't want to have their new shoes delivered to their door? Nick had an idea. He could start the world's largest online shoe store. It was a great idea, but getting the business up and running wouldn't be easy.

Nick purchased a domain name called ShoeSite.com. All he needed were shoes to sell. With zero experience in the shoe industry, he headed to Las Vegas to attend the World Shoe Association show in February 1999. Armed with a business card, Nick shared his business plan with shoe vendors. They thought ShoeSite was interesting, but they weren't convinced to partner up with the new Web site. Nick wasn't willing to give up just yet. He contacted a local shoe store with a proposal: He would post pictures of their shoes on ShoeSite, and if customers ordered, he would drive to the shoe store to pay full price and ship the shoes to the customer. The store owner agreed, and people began ordering shoes from ShoeSite.

More convinced than ever that this dot-com business would be profitable, Nick quit his Autoweb position in June. He devoted his efforts to build ShoeSite but needed investment money. The $150,000 he was able to raise from family and friends wasn't enough. ShoeSite needed larger sums of money and finding a venture capitalist seemed to be the solution. Nick met with a handful of venture capitalists, but they were skeptical. Customers wouldn't want to buy shoes before trying them on, they told him. However, Nick had done his research. In the previous year, one out of two shoes sold were through mail-order catalogs. Still, it wasn't enough to convince the venture capitalists to invest in his online shoe company.

VENTURE FROGS GETS INVOLVED

Nick had one last option—contact a venture capitalist firm called Venture Frogs. They were investing in Internet start-ups. In 1999, Nick called Tony Hsieh and left a detailed message about his ShoeSite. Tony went to erase the voicemail when a statistic caught his attention. According to *Delivering Happiness: A Path to Profits, Passion, and Purpose*, Nick told Tony that "footwear was a $40 billion industry in the United States, and 5 percent of that was already being done by paper mail-order catalogs. It was also the fastest-growing segment of the industry." Tony did the math and realized ShoeSite's financial potential. He saved the message and made an appointment to meet with Nick.

Tony, Alfred, and Nick met in Tony's loft. Although Nick appeared extremely casual in his board shorts and

T-shirt, he was enthusiastic about ShoeSite. Nick noted that e-commerce would most likely continue to catch on with the general public, and no doubt, people would be wearing shoes for a long, long time. Although Tony and Alfred weren't particularly interested in shoes, they liked what they heard. They made two suggestions: find a shoe industry expert and change the company name. Tony thought ShoeSite was limiting. If they wanted to sell other products, they would need a broader company name. Nick suggested "Zapos," taken from the Spanish word *zapatos* meaning "shoes." Tony recommended adding the extra "p" so the name would be properly pronounced. Nick agreed, and Zappos.com was born. Once he found a shoe expert, Nick and the founders of Venture Frogs would meet again.

Nick contacted Fred Mossler, a footwear buyer for Nordstrom. Although Fred was interested, he was not willing to leave his position until Nick could raise additional funds. A meeting was set with Tony, Alfred, Nick, and Fred at a popular diner. While Zappos had been receiving $2,000 worth of orders a week, the profit was used to cover Nick's travel to and from the brick-and-mortar shoe store. This wasn't going to work. If Zappos could develop relationships with the thousands of brands in the shoe industry, then it would have a wider selection to offer its customers. More access meant higher profits. With Fred's contacts in the industry, Nick and Fred believed it would not be difficult to get brands involved with the company. Fred agreed to

Fred Mossler *(pictured on the right)* joined the Zappos team in 1999. As an experienced buyer in the shoe industry, Fred understood the importance of building good working relationships with suppliers.

join Zappos as a senior vice president, and Venture Frogs invested $500,000. The investment gave Zappos a financial cushion through the end of the year and allowed them to pay their employees.

One week later, Fred quit his Nordstrom job and joined Nick at the World Shoe Association show in Las Vegas. Of the eighty shoe brands they spoke with, only three committed to doing business with Zappos. The brands agreed to a drop-ship system, allowing Zappos to send its online orders to each brand's warehouse. In turn, the warehouses would fulfill and ship the orders to a customer using UPS (United Parcel Service). This meant that Zappos would not have the financial burden of running a warehouse or maintaining an inventory. It was an innovative concept in the shoe industry.

Venture Frogs continued adding start-ups to its investments, and Nick was busy growing Zappos. He worked closely with Fred, and together, they checked in with Venture Frogs on a weekly basis. Tony and Alfred reached out to larger venture capital firms. They hoped the firms would eventually buy out Venture Frog's investment in Zappos. One such company was Sequoia Capital. Tony and Alfred were confident Sequoia would want to invest because it had invested in LinkExchange. After all, Sequoia's $3 million in LinkExchange had turned into $50 million in the Microsoft sale.

When he wasn't working, Tony picked up the game of poker. He had played in college, but this time, he was passionate about studying the game. He started to see how similar poker strategies were to business strategies. He discovered that table selection is important as well as knowing how and when to bluff. He learned to be prepared for the worst; to think long-term; to be educated if you're going to play; and to enjoy the process. Many of these lessons Tony drew upon in his work with Venture Frogs and eventually Zappos.

FINDING MOMENTUM

Momentum was starting to build, but despite Venture Frog's initial investment, Zappos was losing money every month. With expensive overhead, they desperately needed to bring on more brands in order to drive online traffic. More brands gave customers a better selection. Nick, Fred, and Tony were doing everything they could think of to make that happen. To add to the pressure, Sequoia Capital had decided not to invest. They thought Zappos was too young but agreed to follow up in a few months. If Zappos didn't get funding fast, the dot-com business would be finished. By mid-December, Venture Frogs had a tough decision to make. Should they invest more money or let Zappos go? If Venture Frogs invested in Zappos again, they wouldn't have enough money to invest in other start-ups. It was a risky decision, but Tony and Alfred were impressed with Nick's passion and commitment to build Zappos for the long-term. Venture Frogs invested for another four months, but there were two conditions. First, Tony was going to be more hands-on. Second, Zappos would need to move into Tony's San Francisco loft since the incubator was still under construction in early 2000. As each four-month period came to an end, Venture Frogs reevaluated their Zappos investment. Each time,

A Chance to Build it Right

According to an online interview with Harvard.edu, Tony recalls what it was like in the early days of LinkExchange. "At LinkExchange, I remember when it was a lot of fun when it was just 5 or 10 of us working around the clock, sleeping under our desks, and having no idea what day of the week it was. But we didn't know to pay attention to company culture, so by the time we were 100 people, the culture of the company had gone completely downhill." Tony dreaded going in to work and thought many of the LinkExchange employees felt the same way.

With Zappos, Tony had the chance to build a company culture the right way. He worked with Nick to create a dynamic, personal, and positive culture built on the organization's core values. He knew that experiences and relationships meant more to him than making money. If this was true for him, then it would be true for others. He could create a fun culture where employees were themselves and were happy to come to work each day. The culture could be fun and well-balanced. Tony reasoned that if the company had a strong relationship with its employees, then Zappos would have a long-lasting and profitable business.

they renewed the investment for another four-month term. This pattern repeated for one year.

During that time, Tony's circle of friends had grown. He reconnected with friends from high school and spent time with friends from college and LinkExchange. Tony deeply valued these relationships and realized that spending time hanging out with these friends made him happy. That year, he threw a big New Year's Eve party. Friends of friends joined him to celebrate the new year, but the fog from the fog machine filled his loft, setting off fire alarms throughout the building. As he watched the flashing lights of fire trucks from the window of his loft, Tony met a mysterious woman. She shared some wisdom that he never forgot. According to *Delivering Happiness*, she said, "Envision, create, and believe in your own universe, and the universe will form around you." Her statement fascinated Tony, and the more he thought about it, he realized he and Alfred had created their own Venture Frogs universe. With Zappos moving in, Tony was excited about the Zappos universe they would build. Tony began spending his days with Nick and the Zappos staff, and eventually became co-CEO in 2001.

ZAPPOS SURVIVAL

Times were tough in the United States in 2000. The dot-com bubble had crashed earlier that year, and Zappos was trying to survive. They were forced to grow slowly

Online retailers have had their fair share of ups and downs, particularly after the crash of the dot-com bubble. However, those who were willing to adapt to the changes typically found financial success.

because of little funding. Venture Frogs invested what was left in its fund and stayed in touch with Sequoia. As an act of financial desperation, Tony began selling off his apartments. He used the money to invest in Zappos. By October 19, 2000, Tony sent out an e-mail to all Zappos employees. It highlighted a nine-month plan focusing on the company's priorities. Zappos couldn't afford the flashy advertising and Web site features of other dot-com companies. What they could do over the next nine months was watch expenses, increase customer orders, boost repeat sales, and count on word-of-mouth referrals. What's more, Zappos was forced to lay off some employees. They asked the remaining staff to work for less money or even for free. Many employees agreed, trading pay for time off or working for stock in the company. Nick needed only enough money to cover expenses including food, transportation, and rent. Even Tony cut his salary to $24 a year before taxes and opened his apartments to house Zappos employees for free. While this kind of "tightening the reins" may have been disheartening for some companies, Zappos employees worked harder than ever. They were committed to seeing the company succeed. Nick and Tony never knew what to expect. Nick told Jay Yarow of BusinessInsider.com, "Okay we got by that obstacle, but now is the inventory going to kill us, or is the bank going to freeze our line of credit or lower the line of credit, which would basically put us out of business. What are we going to do?" Despite what seemed to be a roller-coaster year, Zappos closed out 2000 with thirty employees, over 150 shoe brands, and $1.6 million in gross sales.

THE NEXT STEP

While $1.6 million seemed to be a huge profit, Zappos had high overhead. Nick and Tony had to figure out a way to sell the brands and styles customers wanted. Nick knew that the best company strategy was to give the customers a wide selection and the best service. If customers found what they were looking for and had a good time doing it, they would be back. But how would Nick and Tony make that happen? Zappos would need to buy, stock, and ship its own inventory. This meant the business model needed to change. With Fred Mossler's help, they devised a plan: Hire a buying department, update their Web site, find a warehouse, open a brick-and-mortar store so brands would sell to them, and come up with $2 million to finance the inventory. These tasks seemed doable, but how were they going to raise the money? Tony took a gamble and decided to sell everything he owned.

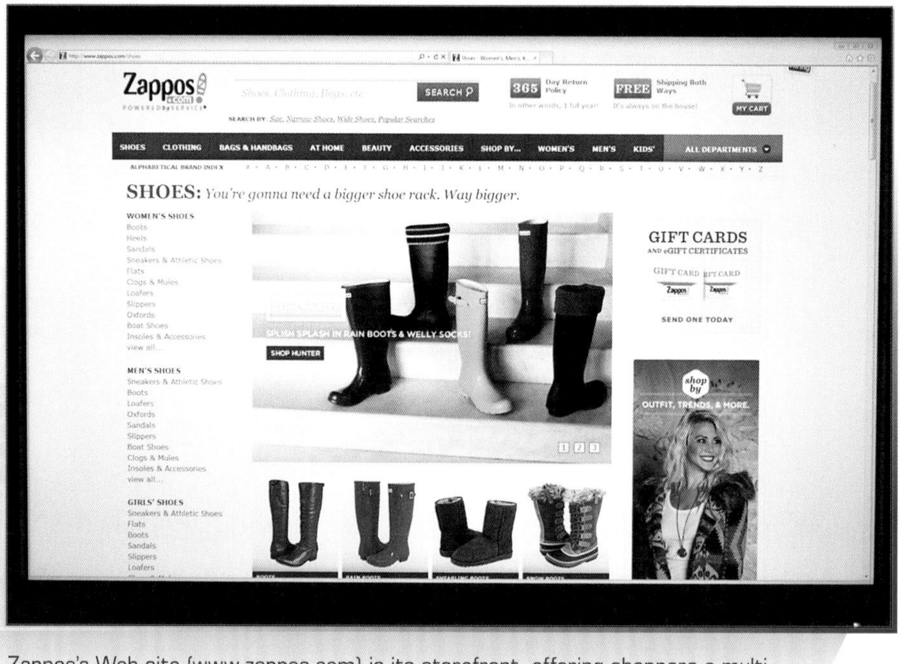

Zappos's Web site (www.zappos.com) is its storefront, offering shoppers a multi-angle view of Zappos products. Customers are able to ask questions, get shopping advice, or find out more about their orders with the click of a button.

One by one, the to-do items were checked off of the list. Zappos opened a temporary brick-and-mortar store in their building until they could find a shoe store that was willing to sell. A small-town shoe store in Willows, California, became available. Zappos bought it, giving the company instant access to more shoe brands. They also rented a 30,000 square foot (2,787 sq meter) abandoned department store across the street. It was perfect for shoe inventory. Zappos moved in and hired new employees. This gutsy move allowed Zappos's sales to more than triple, bringing in $8.6 million in gross sales for 2001. While Nick and Tony were pleased with the progress, much of their profits went to pay for the new inventory.

Chapter 3

If the Shoe Doesn't Fit

Zappos had two ways of getting shoes to their customers: their Willows warehouse and the drop-shipping system with other shoe brands. Both caused problems when it came to getting the right order out to the customer in a timely fashion. The Willows warehouse was not close

Zappos was the first e-tailer to offer free shipping both ways along with a 365-day return policy and 24/7 customer service. Nick and Tony believed that exceptional customer service would win them business.

to a major airport, forcing Zappos to rely on UPS ground shipping. This meant customers had to wait up to a week for their packages. Plus, the drop-ship system was inaccurate. Too often, Zappos customers would make an order only to be told it was on back order or out of stock. What they saw on Zappos's Web site wasn't always available at the brands' warehouse, especially if it was a more popular item. This made it difficult for Zappos to keep up a high level of customer service.

In early 2002, a company called eLogisitics approached Zappos with an idea. Their Kentucky warehouse could help solve Zappos's shipping problems. It was located next to the UPS Worldport hub at the Louisville International Airport. Packages shipped from this location could reach a majority of Zappos customers faster than the Willows location. This would save Zappos a lot of money and would make their customers very happy. Zappos liked the logistics solution and began making plans to move. They would have to transport their inventory from California to Kentucky *and* keep track of online orders. It was no small feat. On Friday, the staff packed forty thousand pairs of shoes into five semitrucks. The trucks drove across the country. By Monday, the inventory needed to be moved into the eLogistics warehouse. By Tuesday, the online orders from the weekend needed to be filled and shipped. It was a good plan until one of the semitrucks overturned, spilling inventory all over the highway. Zappos lost

The Zappos Fulfillment Center in Kentucky is one million square feet (92,903 square meters). This state-of-the-art facility holds an endless assortment of shoes, accessories, apparel, and home goods.

approximately $500,000 worth of retail items.

It didn't take long for problems to arise at eLogistics's warehouse. New merchandise was sitting on the dock still in its packaging. Because it had not been put away on the warehouse shelves, the merchandise could not be included on Zappos's Web site. Zappos was losing tens of thousands of dollars every day. They had to do something quickly. Fred Mossler called Keith Glynn, a go-to Zappos employee. Keith agreed to drop what he was doing at the Willows warehouse and jump on a plane headed for Kentucky. It was leaving in two hours, and Zappos couldn't afford to have Keith go home to pack. He would have to buy what he needed in Kentucky. One week later, Tony and Fred checked in with Keith. The Kentucky warehouse was still not in order. Keith estimated that he would need to stay at least a few more weeks

to get it operational. Nick and Tony stayed in California to handle a bigger problem—Zappos had less than two months of cash to keep the business afloat. Tony asked his real estate agent to sell his loft and told his dad to accept any price. The success of Zappos depended on it.

In July 2002, Tony took a trip to hike and summit the 19,344 feet (5,890 m) of Africa's tallest mountain, Mount Kilimanjaro. He and his friend Jenn Lim had originally planned to take the trip the year prior. However, they had to postpone their travel plans because of the events of September 11, 2001. While Nick and Fred were still working to convince shoe brands to join Zappos, there wasn't much Tony could do but wait for the sale of his loft. He boarded a plane headed for Africa.

Tony Hsieh's 2002 hike took him to the top of Mount Kilimanjaro. The mountain, located just south of the equator, represents almost every ecological system on earth.

Braving the rain, snow, freezing temperatures, and high altitudes, Tony's willpower was tested with every step of the week-long climb. He thought about the comforts of home, his favorite food, and hot showers. He grew to appreciate the people and things in his life on a deeper level. After what seemed to be the most challenging event he'd ever experienced, Tony finally reached the peak of Mount Kilimanjaro. With tears in his eyes, he looked down at the clouds and at the sun, which shined before him. At that moment, he realized anything was possible. When he and Jenn returned home, Tony signed the documents. According to *Delivering Happiness*, Tony sold his loft at 40 percent less than he originally paid. Zappos was saved for another six months.

TAKING CONTROL OF THEIR INVENTORY

During the summer of 2002, Keith Glynn worked to organize the eLogistics warehouse. While he made progress, not all of the orders were filled correctly. Zappos needed another option. Keith found an empty warehouse located within 15 miles (24 kilometers) of the UPS hub. It was in Shepherdsville, Kentucky, and had 50,000 square feet (4,645 sq meters) of space and room to expand. Nick and Tony decided to lease the space, and Keith went back to California to pick up some things from Zappos's headquarters. He loaded his truck, and

Tony joined him for the nonstop, cross-country drive to Kentucky. It took them thirty-six hours—and eighteen energy drinks each—to make it to the new warehouse they called WHISKY, which stood for warehouse inventory system in Kentucky.

Needless to say, eLogistics was not happy with the second Zappos warehouse. Tony proposed an operations competition. Whichever warehouse had the fastest and most accurate shipments in one month would get to store Zappos's entire inventory. Each week that WHISKY beat eLogistics, ten thousand shoes would move to the Zappos warehouse. By the end of the month, the WHISKY warehouse was declared the winner. It was a valuable lesson—never outsource your business's core competency. In other words, eLogistics did not have the same concern for Zappos customers that Zappos did. Tony and Keith did what it took to get WHISKY fully operational, even though neither of them had experience in operating a warehouse. Zappos outgrew WHISKY and worked with the landlord to increase the space. Satisfied with the operation plan they had put into place, Tony returned to San Francisco after five months. Keith stayed for two years before moving back to California.

A PROFITABLE DECISION

The decision to carry Zappos's inventory paid off. In 2002, the company made $32 million in gross sales. Nick and

Tony were excited about the company's success. Tony set a new goal for Zappos to reach $1 billion in gross sales by 2010. It was an ambitious goal, but anything was possible for Zappos. With WHISKY up and running, Nick and Tony took a hard look at another aspect of their business: drop-shipping. According to *Delivering Happiness*, 25 percent of orders were from the drop-ship agreement with other shoe brands. It had been easy money, and Zappos didn't have to be responsible for the inventory. However, drop-shipping was not perfect. This meant Zappos customers were not always getting what they had ordered. In March 2003, Zappos took the plunge. They ended their drop-shipping arrangements with other shoe brands with hopes to carry 100 percent of their inventory. By doing this, Nick and Tony hoped to double their sales in 2003.

Zappos struggled to pay their vendors. With only so much money, they persuaded some vendors to wait for payment. Zappos needed capital, and they needed it fast. They approached Wells Fargo Bank for a $6 million line of credit. It was unheard of for the bank to loan such an amount to an e-tailer, but many of the bank's employees believed in Zappos. One day in June, Tony received a phone call from Wells Fargo Bank. It had taken them two months, but the bank decided to give Zappos the line of credit. Zappos was saved, yet again. The money allowed them to pay their vendors and increase their inventory. In fact, Tony wanted to go from two hundred thousand pairs

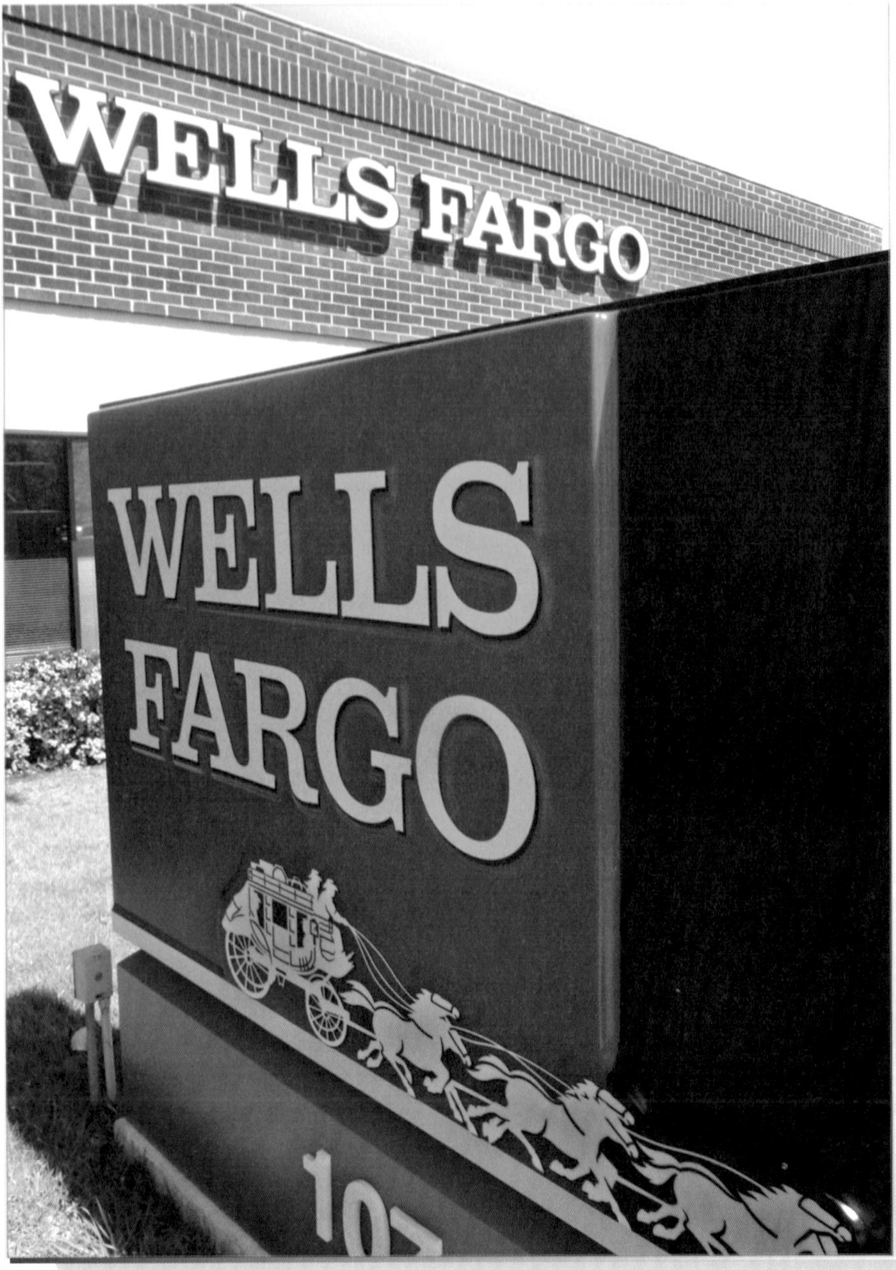

The Wells Fargo headquarters is in San Francisco, California. It is one of the largest banking institutions in the United States with over a trillion dollars in assets.

of shoes to over six hundred thousand by the end of 2004. This ambitious goal would finally allow Zappos customers to shop from the largest shoe selection online, making it the number one dot-com shoe business in the world.

Zappos's Company Culture

Traditionally, company culture is made up of the core values and behaviors practiced by the employees of a company. When communicated properly by those in charge of the company, employees are clear on company goals and function together as a team. Tony believed if the company culture was on the right path, then everything else would fall into place. This would include service, branding, and profits. To him, companies with strong cultures typically surpass those with weak company cultures. He is quoted on Arizona State University's School of Business Web site as saying, "Your culture and your brand are two sides of the same coin."

So what is Zappos's company culture? It's taking time to engage in a Nerf gun battle, a Pinewood Derby car race, an Oreo cookie–eating contest, and a toga parade. It's singing karaoke, dressing up as nerds, making videos, hunting for Easter eggs, and having a flapper night. It's about being yourself and being a little weird. Zappos's culture is about continuing education, teamwork, taking on challenges, and not being afraid to fail. It's about relationships and becoming better people. Although every employee has his or her own interpretation of company culture, at the end of the day, it's about a "work hard and play hard" philosophy. According to Zappos employees, the true magic happens when culture is mixed with an excellent customer experience.

Also in 2003, Tony and Nick took customer service to a new level. They overdelivered using the "WOW factor." Zappos's shoppers would be wowed with a selection that is always in stock. They would also enjoy free shipping, especially free automatic overnight shipping upgrades. It might take a package only eight hours to reach a customer, which was particularly wowing when they were at first told it would take five to six days for delivery. Add a no-fuss money-back guarantee and Zappos customers were so wowed, they told their friends. Although the "WOW factor" would be expensive, Nick and Tony believed the payoff of word-of-mouth marketing would be seen in two or three years.

Zappos was on course, but after a 2003 business meeting, Nick made a decision. He had been sharing the role of co-CEO with Tony since 2001. According to

One may be tempted to wonder if any work gets accomplished in the offices of Zappos.com. With a colorful and casual company culture, Zappos employees work hard and play hard, often at the same time.

Zappos.com, Nick told Tony, "I don't need to be co-CEO. We've gotten to a point now where the CEO's responsibilities are mostly going to be financial, and I don't need the title for my ego." By the time they returned to the office, Nick made an announcement. Tony was going to be the CEO, and Nick would be the chairman. The staff accepted the role change, and business went on as usual. Zappos opened two brick-and-mortar stores and added purses and handbags to go with their designer shoe lines. By the end of the year, gross sales reached $70 million.

ZAPPOS TEAM MEMBERS

The success of Zappos is based on happy employees, or what Zappos calls team members. Nick and Tony knew they needed to create a great work environment where people were encouraged to learn and grow. This meant Zappos needed to hire team members who would fit the company culture. The Zappos hiring process is not easy. Each year, Zappos receives thousands of job applications and only a small percentage of applicants are hired. Recruiters search through the résumés to find candidates with a compatible list of skills, attitude, drive, and passion for helping others. Applicants have to pass two sets of interviews—professional aptitude and culture fit. In other words, the hiring manager wants to know what skills the candidate brings to the table, and the human resources department wants to know "Who would you be if you could be any superhero?" or "What is your theme song?" Many qualified people have been turned down because they were not a good fit for the Zappos culture.

Nick and Tony encourage every team member to live and breathe customer service. This means knowing every aspect of departments that work with customers. Therefore, a month-long training program was designed for all trainees. For the first few weeks, they learn company history, philosophy, and vision. Most important, they get first-hand knowledge of what it means to wow customers by shadowing experienced Zappos Customer Loyalty Team (ZCLT) representatives. Trainees get to work with customers on the phone, answering questions and helping with orders. Then, trainees travel from Nevada to Kentucky to fill orders at the fulfillment center. They call it "KY Boot Camp," and trainees get hands-on experience with the shipping process. Once the training is complete, Zappos's new hires enjoy a graduation ceremony complete with caps and gowns, pictures, and, of course, a party.

Zappos's team member compensation is considered low to average for the call center industry. This is on purpose. Zappos believes team members should be passionate about service, not about their paycheck. To keep team members happy in their positions, Zappos offers paid vacation, sick time, and full medical and dental insurance. To wow team members, Zappos offers pet insurance, a staff discount on Zappos.com, free meals and vending, as well as time in the nap room when needed. At the Kentucky fulfillment center, a library and pool table are provided as well as an area for fitness, karaoke, and video games.

If a team member wants to be promoted, he or she signs up to go through in-house training. For every newly acquired skill, a pay increase is earned. This system motivates team members to continue growing. Other motivation comes from bonuses that are based on culture and peer assessment. Team members give each other Zollars for exceptional behavior in the workplace. Where are Zollars spent? Where else, but in the Zollar Store. Zappos's approach to team member policies has proved to be successful. Their turnover rate is approximately 8.32 percent, well below the rate of other companies like Zappos. If an employee leaves, it's usually because he or she is moving from the area, not because of unhappiness at work. Annual evaluations are based on work performance and adaptation to the Zappos company culture. If an employee no longer fits in well with the culture, it is grounds for dismissal.

THE ZAPPOS CUSTOMER LOYALTY TEAM AND CALL CENTER

While most of Zappos's orders are placed online, on average 6 percent are placed over the phone with the Zappos Customer Loyalty Team (ZCLT). They work in the call center, which functions as the heart and soul of the company. Each day, approximately five thousand phone calls come in from customers who are looking for product advice or have a question about their order. Team members answer the calls using in-house call center software. ZCLT members answer the phones cheerfully, practice good listening skills, and connect with the customer on an emotional level. If trust is built, a onetime caller could become a lifelong Zappos shopper. Tony told Harvard.edu in an online interview:

> I think most people are initially drawn to Zappos because of our huge selection of shoes and clothing, but what creates the passionate loyalty from customers is our focus on customer service. This includes free shipping both ways, our 365-day return policy, our fast shipping, and the fact that we put our 1-800 number at the top of every single page of our Web site because we actually want to talk to our customers. We run our call center pretty differently from most call centers. The goal is to "Deliver

WOW Through Service," so we don't have scripts, call times, or upselling the way most call centers do.

ZCLT members aim to answer all calls within twenty seconds. While the average phone conversation is about five minutes long, Zappos has had a record-breaking phone call that lasted over eight hours. Zappos's goal is to have 80 percent of their ZCLT time in what's called "customer-facing statuses." This means that they are engaging with the customer. The rest of the time is to allow the team member to enjoy a stretch break, handle personal needs, or socialize. They do not require upselling. There are no extra bonuses for sales. ZCLT members have been known to encourage customers to order two sizes of the same shoes if unsure of sizing. In fact, the customer can select the shoes that fit and return the others for a full refund.

If Zappos does not have the exact item a customer is looking for, the ZCLT member will search at least three other competitors' Web sites. If a competitor has the item in stock, then the ZCLT member will direct the caller to the competitor. Zappos may lose the sale, but they'll gain another believer in their exceptional customer service. This type of customer service has been demanding on the bottom line, but over time, it has paid off. By the end of 2003 profits soared, bringing in over $70 million in gross sales.

Chapter 4

On the Move

By the end of 2003, Tony as CEO and Nick as chairman considered moving the Zappos headquarters to another city in the United States. Although it wasn't the cheapest option, Las Vegas seemed to be the most

Las Vegas, where Zappos headquarters relocated in 2004, is known for the bright lights of the Strip, but also for its shopping and entertainment.

promising. Zappos team members could find less expensive housing in Las Vegas than in other cities in the country. Also, there was a better pool of potential employees for the call center. Since Las Vegas was a twenty-four-hour city, it was a perfect fit for Zappos's twenty-four-hour call center. And so it was settled. The ZCLT would move to Henderson, just outside Las Vegas, first and within six months, the rest of the team would follow. Zappos's ninety ZCLT members had a week to decide if they would move. Seventy decided to give it a go.

As time pressed on, the Zappos Web site was looking better than ever. It featured over two hundred shoe brands for men, women, and children. The brand names included Adidas, Birkenstock, Dr. Martens, Nike, and Vans. Even designer brands such as Kenneth Cole, Calvin Klein, Michael Kors, and Isaac Mizrahi joined the Zappos brands. Customers were able to find their favorite shoe brand as each one had its own page on Zappos.com. Photos gave top and side angles, and with a click of a button, customers could get a 360-degree view. In addition, Zappos opened its first outlet store in Kentucky. It seemed that the challenges of building a business were behind Nick and Tony.

In 2004, Sequoia Capital finally decided to invest in Zappos. They gave $35 million, and Zappos used part of the investment to pay team members who had taken payroll cuts in earlier years. In addition, Wells Fargo Bank increased Zappos's credit line to $40 million. Zappos

Zappos's Brand/Culture Pipeline

When Zappos moved to Las Vegas in 2004, they found it difficult to convince their merchandisers and buyers to move, too. They had empty positions that needed to be filled. Tony came up with a two-part plan. First, Zappos would recruit students early in their college careers. By the time they graduated, the recruits would be able to begin their new careers at Zappos. This plan gave Zappos a long-term employment advantage over other recruiting corporations. Second, Zappos would train entry-level team members internally, allowing them the opportunity to advance into higher positions within five to seven years. If a Zappos employee needed to leave, there would always be someone below or above him or her in seniority to cover the workload. This idea became known as Brand/Culture Pipeline (BCP).

Zappos experimented with the BCP strategy in their merchandising department. An entry-level merchandiser was trained, certified, and put into position where he or she could show leadership development. Eventually, that merchandiser would become an assistant buyer, buyer, senior buyer, director, and then a vice president of merchandising. Their experiment worked! Zappos believed in the BCP strategy so much that they put together a Pipeline Team. The team offers courses to help employees grow and become better trained to meet an employment need at the company. The Pipeline's courses range from communication and an introduction to coaching to the science of happiness 101 and stress management. Many of these courses are required for promotion within Zappos.

grossed $184 million in sales and placed as number fifteen on Inc. 500, which is *Inc.* magazine's exclusive ranking of the fastest-growing private companies in the United States.

Zappos team members were so excited about their company culture that they wanted to share it with the world. How could they accomplish that? By putting it in a book. The idea came in 2004, when a group of Zappos team members took a new hire out for a casual meal. Around the table, they shared what the Zappos culture meant to them. Each person had something unique to say. After twenty minutes, they wished the conversation had been recorded for future hires. At the very least, they could write about it, they thought. And so the idea for the *Zappos Culture Book* came to be. Tony requested that every Zappos employee write one or two paragraphs about the Zappos

Jenn Lim, CEO and chief happiness officer of Delivering Happiness, has been a long-time champion of Zappos. She was instrumental in forming the *Zappos Culture Book* and Tony Hsieh's *Delivering Happiness*.

culture. It could include positive or negative feedback, as long as it was honest and confidential. Once collected, the submissions were checked for typos and put together by Jenn Lim. The *Zappos Culture Book* was published in 2005 and since then has been sent to anyone, anywhere in the world, who has requested a copy. And of course, the shipping is free, even if it's sent internationally.

Things were moving along for Zappos in 2005. *Footwear News* had awarded the company the "E-tailer of the Year" Award. In addition, they were beating other brick-and-mortar stores who had developed their own online presence. These companies included Coach, Kmart, Nike, Nordstrom, and Target. They all fell short when compared with Zappos's five hundred brands, sixty thousand styles, and over one million pairs of shoes. Shoppers loved the hassle-free shopping experience, and the orders kept coming in. To handle the orders in the most effective way, Zappos added four hundred team members to cover the growing popularity of their accessories, "vegetarian" footwear, Zappos couture, and designer lines.

Internally, there were also a number of changes. Alfred Lin became the chief financial officer (CFO), and it was time to introduce "the offer." At the end of the first week of training, all new Zappos trainees were offered $100 to quit. This offer was unique in purpose. Tony wanted to be sure every new employee accepted the job for the "right" reason, to be a part of the Zappos culture. The offer was good until the end of training. If the $100 offer was accepted, the candidate would be free to move on to another company, but he or she could never again apply to work at Zappos. Over the years, the offer increased, and by 2011, it reached $4,000. Roughly 2 to 3 percent of trainees have accepted the offer since it first began. With a strong employee force and improvements in 2005, the company gained $370 million in gross sales.

The new year, 2006, ushered in changes for Zappos and especially for Nick. He was ready to move on from Zappos. According to Motoko Rich in the *New York Times*, Nick was tired of "meeting about meetings" and mentioned that "you can only talk about shipping shoes for so long." The article quotes Nick as adding, "But if you take away the culture and keep the free shipping and the free returns, it's the selection and the free shipping that keep the company growing." Nick took the lessons he had learned as Zappos's CEO and chairman and applied them to his new business. He started a custom clothing line called Stagr (pronounced "Stagger"). However, the efforts to keep the business running were more of a challenge than he wanted to handle. After a year, Nick closed Stagr to pursue additional business ventures.

For Zappos, 2006 was a year for expansion. They added a second warehouse in Kentucky, and together, the two warehouses gave Zappos 1,000,000 square feet (92,903 sq

Zappos was created to sell shoes. Today, its higher purpose has become to deliver happiness in other ways. Through customer service and by inspiring other companies, Zappos believes it is sharing happiness worldwide.

meters) of storage. The size is equal to seventeen football fields. With that kind of space, Zappos could house over a thousand brand names in every color, shape, and category. Every morning, delivery trucks drop off shipments to the Zappos fulfillment center. The fulfillment team receives, processes, stocks, and posts each item online for immediate purchase. This keeps the Zappos Web site current and up-to-date with the latest merchandise in their inventory. If the last of a particular item is sold, it is immediately taken off of the Web site. Once a customer places an order, the product is carefully packaged by team members and sealed in a box printed with the Zappos logo. As soon as the Zappos box is taped shut, it is shipped out for delivery. While other companies may wait for the boxes to collect before making a big shipment, Zappos gets the orders out as fast as possible. While it may not be cost effective, Zappos promises customers speedy service.

ZAPPOS CORE VALUES

Companies go through many changes as they grow and learn from their experiences. They learn what is effective and what could be improved upon. This was true with Zappos. With all of their adjustments, one of the most important was the creation of their ten core values. In 2006, Zappos brainstormed to determine which values were most important for them as a company.

Zappos's Core Values:

1. Deliver WOW through service.
2. Embrace and drive change.
3. Create fun and a little weirdness.
4. Be adventurous, creative, and open-minded.
5. Pursue growth and learning.
6. Build open, honest relationships with communication.
7. Build a positive team and family spirit.
8. Do more with less.
9. Be passionate and determined.
10. Be humble.

During training, Zappos candidates learn, memorize, and commit to the core values. Current employees operate in accordance with these values. The values influence their behaviors and, in turn, their behaviors influence actions. The actions give desired results, and this is to make every company decision based on the ten core values, even if the decision adversely affects their profits. These core values helped Zappos reach $597 million in gross sales for 2006.

From the day he suggested changing the company name from ShoeSite to allow for expansion, adding merchandise had always been Tony's goal for Zappos. In 2007, the company reached across the borders of the United States and launched Canada.zappos.com. Although it had a different look, the Canadian Web site offered a great selection and promised customer satisfaction with every delivery, much like its American counterpart. That same year, Zappos acquired 6pm.com, an online footwear and accessories site. Its motto is "Shop. Save. Smile.," and it functioned as an outlet for end-of-the-season Zappos products. The site also sold other merchandise such as clothing, eyewear, children's items, purses, and watches. On a Friday in May 2007, there were a number of 6pm.com shoppers saving and smiling. They were buying up merchandise that had been mismarked. At midnight, a glitch in the pricing engine mistakenly priced all items at $49.95, well below cost according to Eric Engleman of Upstart .bizjournals.com. For six hours, shoppers snapped up the deals. Once team members realized the mistake, they shut down the system to correct the pricing. Regardless, Zappos and 6pm.com honored the $49.95 price, taking a significant financial loss. According to Upstart.bizjournals. com, Tony sent out a tweet saying, "$1.6 million mistake on sister site @6pm.com. I guess that means no ice cream for me tonight." By the end of the year, Zappos made up for the loss by grossing $840 million in sales.

Zappos was looking to the future. No longer were they just in the shoe-selling business. Their Web site now featured everything from accessories to sporting goods. And their efforts didn't stop there. Tony set bold goals for

Zappos and 6pm.com. He wanted the company to reach $1 billion in annual gross sales by 2010.

PERSONAL EMOTIONAL CONNECTION

Tony recognized that Zappos was not just in the merchandise business: it was in the experience business. He wanted the customer experience to involve emotions, connections, making memories, and having a story. This philosophy became a branding promise for the company.

By using new technology, the Zappos fulfillment center is able to ship orders more efficiently and accurately. This addition gives Zappos's customers an exceptional shopping experience.

The ZCLT is encouraged to make a personal emotional connection (PEC) with each customer that phones the call center. This means that team members take time to ask each caller about their day. Sometimes, a customer is having a rotten day and can use a little pick-me-up. One such day came when a woman called Zappos looking for a pair of boots for her husband. She couldn't find them anywhere else and was thrilled when Zappos informed her they had the correct size and brand. The boots were shipped overnight. However, the woman called soon after, explaining her husband had died in a car accident. She needed help returning the boots. A ZCLT member knew how devastating the situation was for the woman and sent her a bouquet of flowers courtesy of Zappos. Although it was an expense for the company, the gesture spoke volumes about the company's desire to focus on the needs of the customer.

While Zappos has many stories of wowing a customer with a PEC, one story speaks to the level of honesty Zappos team members uphold. It involves a woman who had ordered a wallet online. As promised, the wallet was delivered, and after some time, the woman decided to return it. Unknowingly, she had left $150 in the wallet when she sent it back. In the days that followed, she realized she'd lost the money. She accused her children of stealing it. Within a few days, the woman received a note from a Zappos warehouse team member. Inside was the missing money. These PEC opportunities have won the loyalty of Zappos customers all over the country. Just as ZCLT members do special things for their customers, Tony wanted to do the same for the team members. Zappos gave each team member a bonus, which was 10 percent of their annual salary. That year, Zappos profits soared to $840 million in gross sales.

In June 2008, Zappos upgraded the Kentucky fulfillment center with automated conveyors, carousels, and Kiva robots to help fill orders. When an order comes through the Zappos Web site, the high-tech Kiva robots select the item off of a movable shelf and bring it to an employee. It takes only twelve minutes to fill an order, making delivery to the customer faster and more accurate than ever before. These changes have doubled Zappos's shipping efficiency. To add to the excitement, Zappos ran its first television ad campaign. They called it "Put a Little Zappos in Your Day." Its feel-good message told viewers how good it was to get a Zappos package. With colorful graphics and a back-flipping delivery man, the add was supposed to inspire viewers to tap their feet to the fun, upbeat Zappos music and order from Zappos's many brand options.

Even though Zappos was celebrating a big year of development, the party was short-lived. Sequoia Capital warned them of the stock market collapse and housing market depression. They told Zappos to cut expenses and increase their cash flow as quickly as possible. Up to that point, Zappos had spent more money than it was bringing in. Tony was left with one option. In a November 6, 2008, e-mail to all team members, he noted they would have to close some of their Nevada and Kentucky outlet stores and lay off about 8 percent of the staff. The changes would affect almost every Zappos department. Team members who were laid off were given a severance package with health insurance reimbursement for six months and two months worth of pay. For those laid-off team members that had been with Zappos three or more years, they would be getting additional money. It was a difficult decision as many strong friendships had developed over the years. In the end, Zappos moved forward, learning that things are never as good or bad as they seem.

Despite the economic downturn, Zappos received success stories from entrepreneurs and businesses that learned from the Zappos business model. Tony realized that Zappos could teach others about their company culture development, employee practices, and customer service systems. Tony set out to help change the business world, one company at a time. Robert Richman, an entrepreneur already working at Zappos, designed the model that would do just that. It is called Zappos Insights. It was launched in December 2008 and offers online business tools to teach others about culture and core values. If someone wants to become immersed in Zappos, they can sign up for Zappos Insights Live, a two-day seminar. Attendees get to see firsthand the operations at Zappos, hang out with Zappos team members, and network with other business professionals. In addition, Zappos opens it doors for public tours. Tour guides escort visitors through the facility for a free sixty-minute tour, Monday through Friday. If guests are arriving from the airport, a shuttle picks them up for the tour and returns them to their hotel. Once they arrive, guests are able to see Zappos's culture in action.

Chapter 5

Happy Birthday, Zappos!

At the end of 2008, Zappos had just reached its goal of $1 billion in gross sales, two years earlier than the original goal. The layoffs had allowed Zappos to reach its tenth year of business, 2009, with a positive cash flow. There was much to celebrate as Zappos was ranked number twenty-three on *Fortune* magazine's "100 Best Companies to Work For" in February of that year. Tony appeared as a guest judge on NBC's *Celebrity Apprentice* in March. By the end of the year, Venture Frogs was noted as one of the top performing investment funds from 1999, having distributed over 5.8 times the initial fund amount to their investors.

While Zappos was celebrating, Nick Swinmurn was busy starting two new businesses: Stylejuku.com and Dethrone Royalty, Inc. Stylejuku allowed customers to select their favorite items from e-tailers. They then would be able to create outfits and post them for feedback from

Mixed martial arts (MMA) is considered one of the most popular full-contact sports in the world. It combines the techniques of boxing, kickboxing, wrestling, and all types of martial arts.

the Stylejuku community. This business did not enjoy the same longevity or success as Nick's other company, Dethrone Royalty. It showcased an edgy line of clothing and accessories that appealed to fans of mixed martial arts (MMA). It was during his time with Zappos that Nick was introduced to the sport. He had watched every episode of *The Ultimate Fighter*, an American reality television show featuring some of MMA's competitors, on replay. Nick had been hooked. While attending the season two finale, Nick knew he wanted to get involved in the growing popularity of the sport. In 2009, he cofounded Dethrone Royalty, Inc. with his brother Dan. Dethrone Royalty was marketed to MMA fighters and fans, but it took a while for the new company to gather momentum. Nick and Dan had to invest a lot of time, money, and patience to make the brand a success, all lessons Nick had learned while building Zappos.

THE CALL THAT CHANGED IT ALL AT ZAPPOS

After the success of reaching their $1 billion goal, Tony was excited about the direction he was taking Zappos in. He wanted to expand and deliver happiness. However, the

Jeff Bezos is the founder and CEO of Amazon.com, a company he started out of his garage in 1994. What Zappos is to shoes, Amazon is to books. Amazon acquired Zappos in 2009.

board of directors was not excited about his plan. Many wanted a way to regain their investment money and wrap up their commitment to Zappos. Tony and the board were at a crossroads. In order to give the board what they wanted, this meant selling Zappos. In his mind, this was out of the question. The only other solution was to buy out the board members. All he needed was to find $200 million. Then, a phone call from Amazon in early 2009 changed everything.

Vendor Appreciation

Zappos believes that one of the key components to its success is the ongoing relationship they have with their vendors. Because Fred Mossler had already established relationships with many vendors as a Nordstrom buyer, he understood the importance of a mutually beneficial work relationship. The vendors could help Zappos grow and offer better service for its customers. Zappos decided to wow their vendors the same way they wowed their customers. Vendors are greeted at the airport, shuttled to Zappos headquarters, and given refreshments and an on-site tour. This kind of VIP treatment was not the norm in the industry, and Zappos prided itself on building vendor relationships, both personally and professionally. In fact, Zappos took it a step farther. They designed an internal computer program system called the extranet. It gives vendors complete access to Zappos's online inventory and sales figures. Vendors are free to make changes to the way their brand's items are displayed. In fact, the extranet system was helpful to Zappos buyers. Since each Zappos buyer has approximately fifty brands in their portfolio, they appreciate any advice the vendor can offer. Often, this can save time and money whenever a vendor and buyer team up.

Zappos chose to do business with their vendors based on the Golden Rule, which is to treat others as you'd like to be treated. To show appreciation for their vendors, Zappos offered special incentives to vendors who reached their sales goals at Zappos. One such incentive is a T-shirt award. On the front, the T-shirt says, "My brand did a million dollars of sales on Zappos.com." Another incentive is that a Zappos team member will always pay the bill when dining with a vendor at a restaurant. In addition, vendors are invited to participate in a once-a-month golf tournament. But the biggest thank-you Zappos extends is the annual vendor appreciation party. Usually, over one thousand vendors attend to enjoy the food, entertainment, and recognition.

Amazon, the largest online product distribution company, known for its fast order processing and cost-effective shipping, had reached out to Zappos in 2005. At the time, neither Nick nor Tony had been interested in selling Zappos, but they were open to listening. Although Amazon's founder and CEO, Jeff Bezos, had told them he would make Zappos a great offer, it was never presented. Then in 2009, Amazon reached out again, this time offering Zappos a deal that was too good to turn down—$1.2 billion. Excerpts from Tony's July 22, 2009, e-mail to all Zappos employees states the following:

> This morning, our board approved and we signed what's known as a "definitive agreement," in which all of the existing shareholders and investors of Zappos (there are over 100) will be exchanging their Zappos stock for Amazon stock. Once the exchange is done, Amazon will become the only shareholder of Zappos stock. Over the next few days, you will probably read headlines that say "Amazon acquires Zappos" or "Zappos sells to Amazon." While those headlines are technically correct, they don't really properly convey the spirit of the transaction. (I personally would prefer the headline "Zappos and Amazon sitting in a tree...")

The acquisition was final on November 1, 2009. Amazon bought Zappos for four primary reasons: the company had growth potential; their unique culture had led to their past success; their personalized customer service was an asset; and Zappos employees were highly qualified, highly trained people. Amazon and Jeff Bezos thought both companies could learn from each other and benefit their customers. By the time the arrangement was finalized, Zappos was a subsidiary of Amazon. Although there was a new board of directors, Zappos was independent from Amazon. They were free to run their business as they wished, maintaining their quirky culture. Tony received millions of dollars worth of Amazon stock in the deal and agreed to stay on as the CEO. He kept his annual Zappos salary at $36,000. It is his way of being certain he is working at Zappos for one reason: his happiness.

DELIVERING HAPPINESS

A decade ago, Tony had realized his passion for being a part of something bigger than making money. Because he knew that experiences and strong friendships played a big role in his happiness, he began studying the art and science of happiness in 2009. He theorized that there were three levels of happiness: rock star, passion, and higher purpose. The first is short-lived. The second is more engaging, but it lasts only a little longer than the rock star

It all started with an idea. *Delivering Happiness* helps entrepreneurs and businesses develop their organization's principles and values. Pictured here are Jenn Lim and Tony Hsieh.

level of happiness. The final, higher purpose brings the longest-lasting happiness to a person because it stems from a deep-seated meaning. Tony realized the study of happiness helped him, and he encouraged Zappos employees to study it, too. If they can work together to spread happiness, creativity and productivity would thrive at Zappos. Tony extended the company's vision and purpose to "Zappos is about delivering happiness to the world." To share his story with others, Tony put his search for happiness and success into his book *Delivering Happiness: A Path to Profits, Passion, and Purpose.* Tony wrote it with the help of Jenn Lim, the CEO and chief Happiness officer of Delivering happiness. It was published on June 7, 2010, and was number one on the *New York Times* bestseller list for twenty-seven weeks. In addition, *Delivering Happiness* was named one of 2010's best books on business by *Inc.* magazine, National Public Radio (NPR), and the *Wall Street Journal.*

That same year, Tony added more happiness to his plate. Zappos moved up to number fifteen on *Fortune* magazine's "100 Best Companies to Work For" list. On May 1, 2010, Zappos was restructured to form ten companies under the Zappos family of companies. They also announced the opening of a San Francisco office and hired over 1,300 employees.

Chapter 6

The Next Step

Since his time with Zappos, Nick Swinmurn continues to attend board meetings as a Zappos shareholder, keeping a percentage of what he started out with during its early days. He is very involved with Dethrone Royalty, Inc. It has been growing right along with the popularity of MMA. Today, Dethrone Royalty designs all sorts of apparel from hoodies to dresses, hats, and infant wear. They sponsor well-known MMA athletes, and their roster has included Jose Aldo, Phil Davis, Nate Diaz, Nick Diaz, Jon Fitch, Ben Henderson, Ed Herman, Kyle Kingsbury, Josh Koscheck, Gray Maynard, Gilbert Melendez, Charles Oliveira, George Sotiropolous, Joe Stevenson, Cain Velasquez, and Matt Wiman. Outside of MMA, Dethrone Royalty supported boxer Robert Guerrero as well as radio host and truck racer Jason Ellis. They have branched out to sponsor events such as supercross and Baja racing. Their latest endeavor is a sports energy and nutrition beverage called Dethrone Beverage. In 2010, Dethrone Royalty's sales reached just over $1 million. In 2011, its sales reached $1.3 million.

Cain Velasquez, a former UFC heavyweight champion, is one of Dethrone Royalty's sponsored MMA fighters. As a young fighter, Velasquez signed an endorsement deal, agreeing to wear Dethrone Royalty apparel when he is in public.

On July 10, 2012, Dethrone Royalty signed a letter of intent to become a subsidiary of Exclusive Building Services, Inc. Nick Swinmurn and Dan Swinmurn would be on the board of directors under its new corporate name, Dethrone Royalty Holdings, Inc. As an Exclusive Building Services, Inc. subsidiary, Dethrone Royalty will be able to sponsor more extreme athletes as a multisport company.

Besides his work with Dethrone, Nick became a part owner of the Golden State Warriors, a professional basketball team in California, in November 2010. The following November, Nick launched RNKD (pronounced "Ranked"), a company that rewards customers for posting their favorite shoe and clothing brands online. Customers can share what they wear and earn rewards such as gift cards. The idea for RNKD came when he saw a stranger wearing a Dethrone shirt. Being an owner of the brand, he wanted to know more about the people wearing his clothes. He thought other companies might want the same thing.

As an entrepreneur, Nick has enjoyed many successes as well as endured many challenges. Along the way, he has learned many business lessons and is happy to pass on entrepreneurial advice. Professionally, if he has an idea brewing, he shares it with others to see how it sticks. If it has longevity, he names it. Then he figures out the finances and hires a professional team to help him get the idea off of the ground. However, he is quick to point out that all the while, he is dreaming and doubting. According to a

BBC interview, Nick says, "The key is being scrappy. It's the guys that they see an idea and they don't know how they're going [to] do it but they're going to try everything and just fight and claw and keep adapting, keep trying things." Nick also advises entrepreneurs to keep their ego out of the way of business. It's important to stay humble on the road to success.

Although he is busy as an entrepreneur, Nick is a family man. He is married to Gabriela Swinmurn, has one son, and lives in Hillsborough, California. When he isn't working, he drives his son to day care and practices Bikram yoga. While Nick leads a full life, he is still able to communicate with people all over the country, thanks to social media.

Zappos's second core value is "Embrace and drive change." As with any company, change is inevitable. People come and go, and in 2011, Alfred Lin decided to accept a position with their longtime investors, Sequoia Capital. Chris Nielson replaced him as Zappos's CFO and COO.

While Zappos enjoyed doing business with Canadian shoppers, on April 1, 2011, Zappos discontinued its Canadian Zappos site. They felt they could no longer fulfill their first core value, "Deliver WOW through service." Customs rules complicated Zappos fast, free shipping to customers north of the border. Chris Nielson made this announcement on Zappos's CFO and COO blog: "Product selection on Canada.zappos.com is limited due to distribution agreements with the brands we sell in the United States. In addition, we have struggled with the general uncertainty and unpredictability of delivering orders to our Canadian customers given customs and other logistics constraints." Since then, Zappos ships only within the United States, U.S. territories, and military APO/FPO addresses.

Social Media at Work

While most employers frown on the use of social media at work, Tony encourages Zappos team members, called Zapponians, to connect with their customers. This falls in line with one of Zappos's core values: "Build open and honest relationships with communication." Zappos works to be transparent in its branding. This means that they try to be honest with their customers.

The Zappos social media policy is to "be real and use your best judgment." Team members are free to use Zappos's multiple accounts to talk about products, services, and any of the Zappos family of companies. Zapponians can use Facebook, LinkedIn, the Zappos blogs, and Twitter. The company discovered early in its days of social media that one or two Twitter accounts would not accomplish their core value, so they developed their own Twitter microsite. Every month, Zappos enjoys over 1,200 Twitter conversations with customers.

In fact, Tony is one of the most followed people on Twitter, having close to two million followers.

There are a number of ways people can communicate with Zappos. They can add Zappos widgets to their blog, site, or social network. They can also subscribe to Zappos's many blogs including Tony's CEO and COO blog, *Fashion Culture*, *More Than Shoes*, *Zappos.TV*, and *Zappos Family*. In fact, they have specialty blogs for all sorts of interests. From comfort and couture to outdoor and technology, there's something for every Zappos reader. For those with iPads, Zappos presents Zappos Now (ZN). It's a digital magazine iPad app. Readers can stay up on current fashion trends, editorials spreads, products, and travel. YouTube has a collection of Zappos videos, each giving a behind-the-scenes look at the Zappos social media universe. And of course, comments and product feedback are always welcome.

Zappos has been so effective with their social media that other companies have taken notice. Abrams Research, a social media agency, wanted to find out which corporation best used social media. They polled approximately two hundred bloggers, entrepreneurs, and journalists from across the United States and Canada. Zappos took the top spot in 2009.

Change was also on the horizon in Kentucky. With Zappos's growth, it didn't take long before they outgrew their 1,000,000 square feet (92,903 sq meters) of storage at the fulfillment center warehouses. In 2011, Zappos signed a lease for a new warehouse with approximately 118,000 square feet (10,962 sq meters). The warehouse serves as a Zappos returned package center.

MOVING TO DOWNTOWN LAS VEGAS

What had been a thought in late 2009 became a master plan by 2011. Zappos had outgrown its Henderson headquarters. It was ready for a new home. Tony had plans to turn the next Zappos home into a self-sufficient universe. He had studied the campuses of Apple, Google, and Nike. They offered their employees special perks such as free food, basketball courts, video-game rooms, and laundry services. "We realized those campuses were actually really insular and didn't contribute or interact with the community around them," he told T. R. Witcher in an interview for *Time*. "We decided to turn it inside out, and rather than invest in the campus solely, let's invest in the community ecosystem, which will then feed upon itself and become a win-win-win for employees, for Zappos, for local businesses, for the city."

After a diligent search, Tony's plan started with the Las Vegas City Hall building. It is located in downtown

Las Vegas, an area considered to be old and run-down compared to the strip. The city hall building was the perfect location for Zappos's growing staff. Zappos partnered with Resort Gaming Group (RGG), who purchased the city hall for $18 million. Zappos agreed to lease office space from RGG and move in at the end of 2013.

The other part of Tony's plan involved a risky financial investment of $350 million of his own money. A portion would go toward start-ups, another to small businesses to support the community, another to education, and finally, the remainder to real estate development for Zappos employees. Tony understood that the money would transform the downtown area into a community where Zappos team members and their families could live. This meant establishing grocery stores, restaurants, dry cleaners, and real estate offices. More jobs in the downtown Las Vegas area would increase the standard of living and bring a greater sense of community.

Tony told *Inc.* magazine reporter Max Chafkin, "I guess what I'm most excited about is integrating it and bringing people together and making it easy for people who are passionate about it to make it happen. I'd rather just help arrange the different pieces together." In May 2011, Tony rented twenty-five apartments in a brand-new downtown apartment building. Two were used for the downtown project office, twenty were used for hosting business guests,

Zappos headquarters moved to the old city hall building in downtown Las Vegas. This is what the building looked like before renovations.

and the remaining three were combined to make Tony's living space. He knocked down the walls to make a single 5,000 square foot (465 sq meter) residence and set out to customize his new home. He covered the living room walls with plants, hung a framed satellite image of Zappos's future campus, and layered a wall with city planning Post-it notes. To help with entertaining, he installed a pancake machine, shooting out one pancake every few seconds, and an instant mashed potato machine. Tony's goal is to take advantage of the low real estate prices and build a $50 million apartment complex inspired by college dormitory living. Tony was not alone in taking advantage of the low real estate prices. Some of the Zappos employees had followed his lead, including Augusta Scott, the in-house life coach at Zappos. She lives in an apartment just down the hall from Tony.

On February 1, 2012, the Las Vegas City Council finalized Zappos's relocation deal. The plan has inspired the interest of others. More businesses and entrepreneurs are moving to the area. They are ready to join Zappos in developing projects in this area of the city.

2012 Hacking of Zappos

On January 16, 2012, Zappos announced they'd been the victims of a cyberattack. Hackers had illegally accessed one of their servers in Kentucky. They collected names, e-mails, addresses, phone numbers, the last four digits of credit card numbers, and scrambled passwords of over twenty-four million national and international Zappos and 6pm.com customers. Hacking is not a new phenomenon. As long as computers have existed, hackers have attempted to steal important personal and financial information from businesses of every size. According to David Goldman of CNNMoneyTech.com, "Globally, data breaches are expected to have accounted for $130.1 billion in corporate losses last year, according to the Ponemon Institute. Historically, about 30 percent of that total cost has been direct losses attributable to the breaches, which would mean about $39 billion was stolen in 2011." A 2011 credit card cyberattack on Sony affected its seventy-seven million customers. That same year, a thief hacked into 3,400 Citigroup accounts and stole $2.7 million.

In response to the cyberattack, Zappos shut down its customer service phone lines and reset their customers' passwords. They urged their customers to change their log-in data to prevent identity

Since the invention of computers, there have been computer hackers. Here, Brian Coleman, computer forensic examiner, works on several hard drives associated with a crime in 2011.

theft, phishing attacks, and compromised secondary accounts. Zappos worked with the Federal Bureau of Investigation and cautioned customers to be watch out for e-mails or phone calls asking for personal information.

Controversy surrounded Zappos's response to the hacking. Some believed that they had not taken every possible security precaution. In fact, a lawsuit filed by Theresa Stevens against Amazon.com claims that they did not take proper steps to protect their customers' personal information. Stevens's attorney is asking for at least $5 million to cover

(continued on next page)

(continued from previous page)

credit monitoring, identity theft insurance, legal fees, and other expenses. According to securityweek .com, Tony states in a company e-mail, "We've spent over 12 years building our reputation, brand and trust with our customers. It's painful to see us take so many steps back due to a single incident." Tony is convinced Zappos will bounce back, as the company has weathered many storms during its evolution.

COMMUNITY INVOLVEMENT

It's not uncommon for businesses to get involved with charitable organizations, and Zappos is no different. They believe that giving starts at home and developed the Zappos's Wishez program in 2010. It allows employees to make or grant wishes for each other. From warehouse-sized coffee creamer to a car, nothing is too big or too small. At the beginning of 2012, Zappos partnered up with Hope Home Foundation to help its team members purchase homes. Hope Home Foundation is a nonprofit organization that offers financial instruction, coaching, and assistance in making down payments.

Also, Zappos reaches out by participating in many Nevada and Kentucky community events: Nevada Childhood Cancer Foundation, Big Brothers/Big Sisters, West Coast Conference Kids Day, Aid for AIDS Nevada (AFAN),

Participants in the Rock 'n' Roll Las Vegas Marathon & ½ Marathon take on the city's famous Strip. The course is lined with stages featuring live music from well-known musicians, such as Bret Michaels *(above)*.

Hannah's Socks, the Center for Women and Families, and the Shade Tree Women's Shelter. They have partnered with companies such as Bearpaw and Steve Madden 4 The Cool People. In addition, Zappos reaches beyond its borders to help international causes such as charity:water. This organization delivers water to people who do not have access to safe drinking water.

Since 2009, they sponsored the Zappos.com Rock 'n' Roll Las Vegas Marathon & ½ Marathon on the Las Vegas Strip. Also that year, they signed three-year title sponsorship deals with the West Coast Conference (WCC) men's and women's basketball championships. They partnered with Soles4Souls to encourage the eight participating WCC colleges to collect as many new shoes as possible from December to the end of the basketball season. Donations go toward those in need around the world. In addition, Soles4Souls and Zappos.com donated new shoes to at-risk children from the Clark County School District and the Las Vegas After School All-Star program. In 2010, they gave $150 Zappos.com gift certificates to each of the five hundred students at Bullitt Lick Middle School in Kentucky. From toy drives to providing medical supplies, assisting at family shelters, and donating thousands of pairs of shoes, Zappos and its employees try to help others. Zappos's community involvement helped the company reach number six in 2011 in *Fortune* magazine's list of "Best Companies to Work For."

TONY HSIEH TODAY

Because of the many career-related projects he is interested in, Tony is focused on work. He remains single and does not define "dating" in the traditional sense of the word. He prefers hanging out and maintains many close-knit friendships. "My view is that I am more of a mirror of who I am around," he said to a *New York Times* reporter. "So if I am around an introverted person that is really awkward. But if I am around an extroverted person I will be whoever they are times point-5." The article went on to

Nick Swinmurn's dream to create an online shoe store became a reality with Zappos.com. Although he left the company for other opportunities, he continues to practice many of the customer service principles he applied at Zappos.

note that Tony has a form of social phobia. However, according to Antonio Dodge, a personality assessment consultant, he doesn't let it stop him from being social.

Like Nick Swinmurn, Tony Hsieh has experienced many entrepreneurial ups and downs through the years. He is always ready to share the lessons he's learned. Tony encourages entrepreneurs to think big and to find ways to merge personal passions with professional goals. Customers are always king and should be wowed with respect and appreciation. Tony believes that choosing where to get involved in business is the most important decision. And finally, he encourages entrepreneurs to envision, create, and believe in their passion. When they do, they have the potential to become as successful as Zappos, a billion-dollar dot-com business that prides itself on customer satisfaction and happy employees.

Fact Sheet on
Nick Swinmurn

Full Name: Nicholas Swinmurn

Date of Birth: 1973

Birthplace: England

Current Residence: California

Marital Status: Married to Gabriela Swinmurn

Children: One son

College attended: University of California, Santa Barbara (bachelor of film studies)

First Job: Bicycle club and tennis club

Titles held: Group ticket sales for San Diego Padres (1996)
Sales marketing manager for Autoweb.com (1997–1998)
Founder and CEO of Zappos.com, Inc. (1998–2001)
Co-CEO of Zappos.com, Inc. (2001–2003)
Chairman of Zappos.com, Inc. (2003–2006)
Founder of Stylejuku.com (2009)
Cofounder of Dethrone Royalty Holdings, Inc. (2009–present)

Fact Sheet on

Tony Hsieh

Full Name: Tony Hsieh

Date of Birth: December 12, 1973

Birthplace: Illinois

Current Residence: Las Vegas, Nevada

Marital Status: Single

Children: None

College attended: Harvard University (bachelor of computer science)

First Job: Earth worm distributor (1982)

Titles held: Comanager at Quincy House Grille (1994–1995)
Software engineer at Oracle Corporation (1995–1996)
Cofounder of LinkExchange (1996–1998)
Cofounder Venture Frogs (1998–present)
Investor in Zappos.com, Inc (1999–present)
Co-CEO of Zappos.com, Inc. (2001–2003)
CEO of Zappos.com, Inc. (2003–present)

Fact Sheet on

Zappos.com, Inc.

Date launched: 1999

Founded by: Nick Swinmurn

Operated under: ShoeSite.com (1998)
Zappos.com, Inc. (1999–present)

Mantra: Zappos is about delivering happiness to the world.

Headquarters: Henderson, Nevada

Number of employees: Over 2,700

Zappos family: Zappos CLT, Inc.
Zappos Development, Inc.
Zappos Retail, Inc.
Zappos Fulfillment Centers, Inc.
Zappos Gift Cards, Inc.
Zappos Insights, Inc.
Zappos IP, Inc.
Zappos Merchandising, Inc.
Zappos.com, Inc.
6pm.com, LLC

Timeline

1973 Nicholas (Nick) Swinmurn is born in England.

December 12, 1973 Tony Hsieh is born in Illinois.

1980 The Swinmurn family moves to the San Francisco Bay area of California.

1982 Tony starts an earthworm distribution business as a nine-year-old.

1994–1995 Tony runs a pizza business with Sanjay Madan at Quincy House Grille on the Harvard campus.

1995 Tony graduates from Harvard University.

1995 Tony and Sanjay Madan take jobs at Oracle Corporation in California.

March 1996 Tony and Sanjay Madan launch LinkExchange.

1996 Nick graduates from the University of California, Santa Barbara.

1996 Nick sells group tickets for the San Diego Padres, a professional baseball team in California.

August 1996 LinkExchange receives an offer to sell for $1 million.

December 1996 Yahoo! makes an offer to buy LinkExchange for $20 million.

1997 Nick becomes the sales marketing manager for Autoweb.com.

1997 Ali Partovi joins LinkExchange as a computer programmer and partner.

May 1997 Sequoia Capital invests $3 million dollars in LinkExchange.

1997 Alfred Lin joins LinkExchange as VP of finance.

1998 Tony quits LinkExchange to pursue other interests.

1998 Nick comes up empty-handed from a shopping trip. He researches the shoe industry.

1998 LinkExchange hires over a hundred employees.

November 1998 Microsoft buys LinkExchange for $265 million.

February 1999 Nick attends the World Shoe Association show in Las Vegas.

1999 Nick buys the domain name ShoeSite.com.

June 1999 Nick quits his position at Autoweb.com.

August 1999 Tony moves into a loft in the Marquee Historical Building in San Francisco.

1999 Tony and Alfred launch Venture Frogs.

1999 Nick contacts Tony Hsieh at Venture Frogs.

1999 Fred Mossler quits Nordstrom to join Zappos.

1999 Nick and Fred attend the World Shoe Association show in Las Vegas.

1999 Venture Frogs invests $500,000 in the company.

1999 Zappos claims selection as their vision and brand.

1999 Zappos has minimal profits.

December 1999 Venture Frogs invests more money, bringing their total to $1.1 million.

Early 2000 Zappos moves into Venture Frog's loft.

2000 The dot-com bubble bursts.

October 19, 2000 Tony sends a company-wide e-mail explaining Zappos's nine-month plan.

2000 Zappos reaches $1.6 million in gross sales.

2001 Tony Hsieh joins Nick as co-CEO at Zappos.

2001 Zappos changes it business model and works to raise $2 million for inventory.

2001 Tony decides to sell his real estate to reinvest in Zappos.

2001 Zappos buys a shoe store and rents a warehouse for its inventory in Willows, California.

2001 Zappos reaches $8.6 million in gross sales.

Early 2002 Zappos opens the Kentucky fulfillment center.

Summer 2002 Keith Glynn works to get the fulfillment center up and running.

2002 Zappos reaches $32 million in gross sales.

March 2003 Zappos decides to distribute 100 percent of its own inventory by canceling their drop-shipping arrangement with other brands.

2003 Zappos makes customer service a company focus.

June 2003 Wells Fargo Bank gives Zappos a loan of $6 million.

June 19, 2003 Tony makes plans to increases inventory from two hundred thousand to six hundred thousand pairs of shoes.

2003: Nick gives up position as co-CEO.

2003: Zappos reaches $70 million in gross sales.

2003: Two brick-and-mortar Zappos stores are opened.

End of 2003 Nick and Tony consider moving Zappos headquarters to another city.

April 2004 Zappos moves its headquarters from San Francisco, California, to Henderson, Nevada.

2004 Sequoia Capital invests approximately $35 million in Zappos.

2004 Zappos is number fifteen on the Inc. 500, which is *Inc.* magazine's ranking of the fastest-growing private companies in the United States.

2004 Zappos reaches $184 million in gross sales.

2004 The first Zappos outlet store opens in Kentucky.

2005 Zappos publishes its first *Culture Book*.

2005 Tony hires Venture Frogs cofounder Alfred Lin to be Zappos's CFO.

2005 The Zappos site offers nearly sixty thousand styles of footwear for men, women, and children.

2005 Zappos introduces "the offer" to trainees. (The amount increases over the years.)

2005 *Footwear News* awards Zappos the "E-tailer of the Year" Award.

2005 Culture and core values becomes Zappos's platform.

2005 Zappos reaches $370 million in gross sales.

2006 Nick leaves Zappos and starts a custom apparel line called Stagr.

2006 Zappos moves to a larger fulfillment center in Shepherdsville, Kentucky.

2006 Zappos reaches $597 million in gross sales.

2007 Nick closes Stagr.

2007 Zappos launches its Canadian site, Canada.zappos.com.

2007 Zappos acquires 6pm.com from eBags.com.

2007 Zappos adds new merchandise categories to Zappos.com.

May 2007 Zappos honors 6pm.com mismarked merchandise and loses $1.6 million.

2007 Zappos adds personal emotional connection (PEC) to its platform.

2007 Tony begins to study the art and science of happiness.

2007 Zappos reaches $840 million in gross sales.

2008 Zappos publicizes its first TV ad campaign, "Put a Little Zappos in Your Day."

July 2008 The Zappos fulfillment center in Kentucky gets an upgraded system using automated conveyors, carousels, and Kiva robots.

November 2008 Zappos cuts back on expenses, lays off 8 percent of staff, and closes some of their Nevada and Kentucky outlet stores.

December 2008 Zappos launches ZapposInsights.com.

2008 Zappos achieves their goal of over $1 billion in gross merchandise sales.

2009 Zappos reaches its tenth year in business.

February 2009 Zappos is ranked number twenty-three on *Fortune* magazine's "100 Best Companies to Work For" list.

March 2009 Tony appears as a guest judge on NBC's *Celebrity Apprentice*.

March 2009 Nick starts Dethroned Royalty, Inc., a new clothing brand.

2009 Abrams Research awards Zappos the "best use of social media."

July 2009 Tony announces Amazon is buying Zappos.

2009 Amazon acquires Zappos for over $1.2 billion at closing.

2009 Zappos expands their purpose and vision: "Zappos is about delivering happiness to the world."

2009 Zappos sponsors the Rock 'n' Roll Las Vegas Marathon & 1/2 Marathon.

End of 2009 Venture Frogs becomes one of the top-performing venture capitalist funds by distributing over 5.8 times the initial fund amount to its investors.

2010 Zappos is ranked fifteen on *Fortune* magazine's annual "100 Best Companies to Work For" list.

May 1, 2010 Zappos restructures the company into ten separate companies under the Zappos family of companies.

2010 Zappos starts the Wishez employee program.

November 2010 Nick becomes one of the owners of the Golden State Warriors, a professional basketball team in California.

2010 Dethrone Royalty's gross sales reach just over $1 million.

Early 2011 Alfred Lin leaves Zappos to work with Sequoia. Chris Nielson replaces him as Zappos's CFO and COO.

2011 Zappos is sixth on *Fortune* magazine's "100 Best Companies to Work For" list.

April 1, 2011 Zappos shuts down Canada.zappos.com.

2011 Tony makes plans to move the Zappos headquarters to city hall in downtown Las Vegas.

2011 Zappos increases "the offer" to $4,000 for trainees.

May 2011 Tony rents twenty-five apartments in a brand new downtown Las Vegas apartment building.

November 2011 Nick Swinmurn launches RNKD.

2011 Dethrone Royalty's gross sales reach $1.3 million.

2011 Zappos signs a lease to add almost 118,000 square feet (10,962 sq meters) to their warehouse space in Kentucky. The lease was for a Shepherdsville's Cedar Grove Business Park warehouse that would function as a return center.

January 16, 2012 Zappos announces one of its servers in Kentucky was hacked.

February 1, 2012 The Las Vegas City Council finalizes Zappos's relocation deal.

2012 Zappos partners up with Hope Home Foundation to help its team members find homes.

Glossary

acquisition The process of one company buying most or all of another.

back order A customer's order that cannot be filled because of a temporary lack of supply.

brand A product line of goods or services.

branding A company's identity noted with a reoccurring logo, color, trademark, or name.

brick-and-mortar A term describing a retail store located in a building, as opposed to online.

board of directors The governing body of a company that represents the shareholders.

call center A location that accepts business calls from customers.

capital The money or property that represents the wealth of an individual or business.

capital-intensive business A business that needs large amounts of money to operate.

core values Principles that reveal a company's highest priorities for conduct and business.

crowdsourcing The practice of working as a group to accomplish a goal or complete a project.

dot-com bubble The name for the 1990's dot-com stock boom.

dot-com business A business that offers products and services using the Internet. The ".com" stands for "commercial."

drop-ship A system allowing a business to send orders to another company to fulfill and ship the order to the customer.

e-commerce The buying and selling of goods and services online.

entrepreneur A person who builds and assumes responsibility for a business venture.

e-tailer An online company that sells goods and services.

gross sales The total amount of sales before deducting discounts, product returns, and taxes.

human resources The division of a company that handles employee recruiting, training, and benefits.

identity theft The act of stealing another's identity to access personal or financial information.

internet start-up A young online company, typically looking for financial backing.

inventory A business's finished or unfinished products that have yet to be sold.

layoffs The act of suspending or dismissing an employee because of a lack of work or money.

overhead The added expenses of running a business such as rent, shipping, returns, utilities, taxes, materials, and labor.

phishing attacks The criminal act of sending e-mails in hopes of receiving personal and banking information for financial gain.

pipeline When referring to employment practices, trained employees that can assume an open position within a company.

public company A business that sells its shares to the public to raise money.

relationship marketing The strategy of building a long-term relationship with customers.

severance package Compensation given to employees that have been laid off. It can include payment, stocks, and other benefits.

shareholder A person or body that owns at least one share of a company.

stock market A place where stocks are bought, sold, or traded.

subsidiary A business under the control of a parent company that owns more than 50 percent of its stock.

turnover The number of employees hired to replace those who have left during the course of a year.

upselling An attempt to get customers to buy more than what they intended.

vendor A company that sells goods or services to another company.

venture capitalist A private investor who gives capital and business advice to promising start-ups in order to sell their shares for a higher profit.

word-of-mouth marketing A customer's recommendation of a company to another prospective customer.

For More Information

Amazon.com, Inc.
1516 2nd Avenue
Seattle, WA 98101
(206) 622-2335
Web site: http://www.amazon.com

Amazon.com, Inc. is one of the largest online e-tailers with Web sites servicing the United States, Canada, China, France, German, Italy, Japan, Spain, and the United Kingdom. Amazon sells everything from books and electronics to jewelry and computer software. Amazon acquired Zappos in 2009.

Delivering Happiness, LLC
8022 S. Rainbow Boulevard, Suite 394
Las Vegas, NV 89139
(774) 277-9750
Web site: http://www.deliveringhappiness.com

Delivering Happiness brings people committed to happiness together. They teach individuals and businesses the science of happiness using products, educational programs, online information, and speaking events.

Dethrone Royalty Holdings, Inc.
415 San Raymundo Road
Burlingame, CA 94010
Web site: http://www.dethrone.com
Dethrone Royalty is a clothing and accessory company founded by Nick Swinmurn in March 2009. Its main customer base is made up of MMA fans in the United States, Australia, and Canada.

Harvard University
Harvard Yard
Massachusetts Hall
Cambridge, MA 02138
(617) 495-1000
Web site: http://www.harvard.edu
Harvard University is where Tony Hsieh earned his undergraduate degree in computer science. It is also where he honed his entrepreneurial skills and met future business partners Sanjay Madan and Alfred Lin.

6 pm.com, LLC
2280 Corporate Circle, Suite 100
Henderson, NV 89074
(888) 676-2660
Web site: http://www.6pm.com
Zappos acquired 6pm.com from eBags.com in 2007. 6pm.com functions as an online outlet store for

end-of-the-season Zappos merchandise such as apparel, handbags, and shoes.

Zappos.com, Inc.
2280 Corporate Circle
Henderson, NV 89074
(800) 927-7671
Web site: http://www.zappos.com
Zappos, an Amazon subsidiary, is an online e-tailer of shoes, apparel, home goods, beauty supplies, and electronics. Nick Swinmurn founded the company in 1999 and with Tony Hsieh's investment and know-how, the two grew the business into what it is today. Tony continues to function as the CEO while Nick serves as a shareholder.

Zappos Fulfillment Center
376 Zappos.com Boulevard
Shepherdsville, KY 40165
(502) 921-4901
Web site: http://about.zappos.com/zappos-story/fulfillment-facility
The state-of-the-art fulfillment center is dedicated to the distribution of Zappos merchandise. They use automated conveyors, carousels, and Kiva robots to help team members deliver merchandise to customers quickly and efficiently.

Zappos Insights, Inc.
2280 Corporate Drive, Suite 100
Henderson, NV 89074
1 (877) 513-7424
Web site: http://www.zapposinsights.com
Zappos Insights offers events, tours, and monthly memberships to mentor business professionals from the United States, Canada, and Europe. Zappos Insights helps others create more effective business cultures, core values, and customer service systems.

WEB SITES

Due to the changing nature of Internet links, Rosen Publishing has developed an online list of Web sites related to the subject of this book. This site is updated regularly. Please use this link to access the list:

http://www.rosenlinks.com/IBIO/Zapp

For Further Reading

Ben-Shahar, Tal. *Happier: Learn the Secrets to Daily Joy and Lasting Fulfillment*. New York, NY: McGraw-Hill, 2007.

Collins, Jim. *Good to Great: Why Some Companies Make the Leap...and Others Don't*. New York, NY: HarperCollins, 2001.

Conley Chip. *Emotional Equations*. New York, NY: Free Press, 2012.

Conley, Chip, and Tony Hsieh. *Peak: How Great Companies Get Their Mojo from Maslow*. San Francisco, CA: Jossey-Bass, 2007.

Dennis, Felix. *How to Get Rich*. New York, NY: Penguin Group, 2006.

Ferriss, Timothy. *4-Hour Work Week: Escape 9-5, Live Anywhere, and Join the New Rich*. New York, NY: Crown Publishers, 2009.

Ford, Lisa, David McNair, and William Perry. *Exceptional Customer Service: Exceed Customer Expectations to Build Loyalty and Boost Profits*. Avon, MA: Adams Business, 2009.

Gilbert, Daniel Todd. *Stumbling on Happiness*. New York, NY: Vintage Books, 2005.

Gladwell, Malcolm. *Outliers: The Story of Success*. New York, NY: Little, Brown and Company, 2008.

Gladwell, Malcolm. *The Tipping Point: How Little Things Can Make a Big Difference*. Boston, MA: Little, Brown and Company, 2002.

Godin, Seth. *The Dip: A Little Book That Teaches You When to Quit (and When to Stick)*. New York, NY: Penguin Group, 2007.

Goldsmith, Marshall, and Shane Clester. *What Got You Here Won't Get You There: A Round Table Comic: How Successful People Become Even More Successful*. Mundelein, IL: Writers of the Round Table Press, 2011.

Haidt, Jonathan. *The Happiness Hypothesis: Finding Modern Truth in Ancient Wisdom*. New York, NY: Basic Books, 2006.

Heath, Chip, and Dan Heath. *Made to Stick: Why Some Ideas Survive and Others Die*. New York, NY: Random House, 2008.

Hsieh, Tony. *Delivering Happiness: A Path to Profits, Passion, and Purpose*. New York, NY: Hachette Book Group, 2010.

Hsieh, Tony, and Rob Ten Pas. *Delivering Happiness: A Path to Profits, Passion, and Purpose; A Round Table Comic*. Mundelein, IL: Round Table Companies, 2012.

Ishizuka, Shinobu. *The Zappos Miracle*. Los Angeles, CA: Dyna-Search, 2010.

Johnson, Spencer. *Who Moved My Cheese?: An Amazing Way to Deal with Change in Your Work and in Your Life*. New York, NY: G. P. Putnam's Sons, 2002.

Logan, David, and John King. *Tribal Leadership: Leveraging Natural Groups to Build a Thriving Organization*. New York, NY: HarperCollins, 2008.

Margolis, Michael. *Believe Me: Why Your Vision, Brand, and Leadership Need a Bigger Story*. New York, NY: Get Storied Press, 2009.

Michelli, Joseph. *The Zappos Experience: 5 Principles to Inspire, Engage, and WOW*. New York, NY: The McGraw-Hill Companies, 2012.

Reichheld, Fred. *The Ultimate Question: Driving Good Profits and True Growth*. Boston, MA: Harvard Business School Publishing, 2006.

Sanborn, Mark. *The Fred Factor: How Passion in Your Work and Life Can Turn the Ordinary into the Extraordinary!*. Colorado Springs, CO: WaterBrook Press, 2002.

Seligman, Martin. *Flourish: A Visionary New Understanding of Happiness and Well-Being*. New York, NY: Free Press, 2011.

Solis, Brian. *The End of Business as Usual: Rewire the Way You Work to Succeed in the Consumer Revolution*. Hoboken, NJ: John Wiley & Sons, 2012.

Zappos. *Zappos.com 2011 Culture Book*. City of Industry, CA: Orbitel International LLC, 2011.

Bibliography

Ayres, Ian. "Paying People to Quit: What Law Schools Can Learn from Zappos." Freakonomics.com, 2011. Retrieved May 28, 2012 (http://freakonomics.com/2011/11/21/).

BBC. "BBC: News Business Interview with Nick Swinmurn." BBC.com, 2010. Retrieved May 12, 2012 (http://www.bbc.co.uk/news/10323197).

Bloomberg Business Week. "Amazon Buys Zappos.com for $847M in Stock, Cash." 2009. Retrieved June 3, 2012 (http://www.businessweek.com/bwdaily/dnflash/content/jul2009).

Cass, Meghan. "Zappos Milestone: Q&A with Nick Swinmurn." Footwear News at Zappos.com, 2009. Retrieved May 12, 2012 (http://about.zappos.com/press-center).

Chafkin, Max. "Tony Hsieh's Excellent Las Vegas Adventure." *Inc.*, 2012. Retrieved May 13, 2012 (http://www.inc.com/magazine/201202).

Engleman, Eric. "Error Costs Amazon Unit $1.6 Million." *Upstart Business Journal*, 2010. Retrieved July 25, 2012 (http://upstart.bizjournals.com/news/technology/2010/05/24).

Goldman, David. "Zappos Hacked, 24 Million Accounts Accessed." CNNMoneyTech.com, 2012. Retrieved May 13, 2012(http://money.cnn.com/2012/01/16/technology/zappos_hack/index.htm).

Harvard University School of Engineering and Applied Sciences. "Tony Hsieh." Retrieved May 15, 2012 (http://www.seas.harvard.edu/news-events/publications).

Hsieh, Tony. *Delivering Happiness: A Path to Profits, Passion, and Purpose*. New York, NY: Hachette Book Group, 2010.

Juanne. "Dethrone Royalty Launches New Sports Nutrition Beverage." MMA Hype, 2012. Retrieved July 18, 2012 (http://www.mmahype.co.za/2012/06/dethrone-royalty-launches-new-sports-nutrition-beverage/).

Karman, John, III. "Zappos Adds 1,300 Workers, Outgrows Space." *Business First*, 2011. Retrieved June 4, 2012 (http://www.bizjournals.com/louisville/print-edition).

Know WPC. "Zappos CEO Tony Hsieh: Customer Focus Key to Record Sales During Retail Slump." Arizona State University W. P. Carey School of Business, 2009. Retrieved July 25, 2012 (http://knowledge.wpcarey.asu.edu/article.cfm?articleid=1736).

Miller, Paige. "Zappos, Inc. Move to Downtown Las Vegas Expected to Boost Economy, Revitalize Downtown." Smart Growth America, 2012. Retrieved June 3, 2012 (http://www.smartgrowthamerica.org/2012/03/15/).

Nielson, Chris. "Canada.zappos.com." Zappos blogs: CEO and COO blog, 2011. Retrieved July 19, 2012 (http://blogs.zappos.com/canadazapposcom).

Reinsmith, Trent. "UFC on FOX 1: BR MMA Interview with Dethrone Royalty Founder Nick Swinmurn." *Bleacher Report*, 2011. Retrieved May 15, 2012 (http://bleacherreport.com).

Rhodes, Nelson. "Zappos.com, Inc." Reference for Business. Retrieved July 20, 2012. (http://www.referenceforbusiness.com/history/Vi-Z/Zappos-com-Inc.html).

Rich, Motoko. "Why Is This Man Smiling?" *New York Times*, 2011. May 15, 2012 (http://www.nytimes.com/2011/04/10/fashion/10HSEIH.html?pagewanted=all).

Wallace, Rob, and Marc Dorian. "More Than Money: Surprising Stories of the Superrich And How They Gave Back." Abcnews.com, 2011. Retrieved May 12, 2012 (http://abcnews.go.com/Business/surprising-stories-superrich-gave-back/story?id=14826520#2).

Witcher, T. R. "The Billionaire Who Wants to Remake Downtown Las Vegas." *Time*, 2012. Retrieved May 12, 2012 (http://www.time.com/time/nation/article/0,8599,2112157,00.html).

Yarow, Jay. "The Zappos Founder Just Told Us All Kinds Of Crazy Stories—Here's The Surprisingly Candid Interview." Businessinsider.com, 2011. Retrieved May 12, 2012 (http://articles.businessinsider.com).

Index

A

B

D

E

G

H

L

ABOUT THE AUTHOR

While researching this book Erin Staley realized that she had a passion for entrepreneurship and became a partner and editor for an online Puerto Vallarta magazine. Staley enjoys writing nonfiction books for teens, jewelry making, going to the theater, and watching the ocean waves roll onto Mexico's golden shores.

PHOTO CREDITS

Cover (left), pp. 3 (left) 10, 16, 47, 73, 83, 93, 97 © AP Images; cover (right), pp. 3 (right), 12, 25, 38, 50–51, 74–75 Bloomberg /Getty Images; pp. 7, 95 Ethan Miller/Getty Images; p. 13 Zoonar /Thinkstock; p. 23 William Widmer/Redux; p. 29 Dimitrios Kambouris/Getty Images; p. 34 Chris Hondros/Getty Images; p. 36 Karen Bleier/AFP/Getty Images; pp. 40–41 Tyler Bissmeyer/The New York Times/Redux; pp. 42–43 Hemera /Thinkstock; p. 56 Emmanuel Coupe/Photographer's Choice /Getty Images; p. 60 Michael Loccisano/Getty Images; p. 63 © Ruaridh Stewart/ZUMA Press; p. 67 Brett Humphreys/ Redux; p. 80 Michael Bezjian/WireImage/Getty Images; pp. 90–91 Isaac Brekken/The New York Times/Redux; background image pp. 21, 22, 32, 48, 49, 58, 59, 76, 77, 86, 87, 92, 93, 94 kentoh/Shutterstock.com; cover and remaining interior background image dpaint/Shutterstock.com.

Designer: Brian Garvey; Editor: Bethany Bryan;
Photo Researcher: Marty Levick